SO MUCH BAD
IN THE BEST OF US

SO MUCH BAD IN THE BEST OF US

The Salacious and Audacious Life of John W. Talbot

—⚭—

GRETA FISHER

RED ⚡ LIGHTNING BOOKS

This book is a publication of

Red Lightning Books
1320 East 10th Street
Bloomington, Indiana 47405 USA

Redlightningbooks.com

Manufactured in the United States of America

First printing 2022

Cataloging information is available from the Library of Congress.

ISBN 978-1-68435-187-9 (hardback)
ISBN 978-1-68435-188-6 (paperback)
ISBN 978-1-68435-189-3 (ebook)

For Amy, Rachel, and Rowan, who never stop asking questions

CONTENTS

ACKNOWLEDGMENTS

THANKS TO ALL THOSE who encouraged me to keep investigating and shared my enthusiasm for this strange and remarkable tale. Particular thanks to Lauren Kunstman, who tirelessly asks what motivates the actions that become our history and never seems to run out of new places to look for clues; Margaret Fosmoe, who always loves a good story; and Toni and Jonathan Cook, whose ties to the Owls run deep.

SO MUCH BAD
IN THE BEST OF US

INTRODUCTION

If you have for sale something the people want, they will make you rich.

—John W. Talbot, *Old Maid Ryan*

THE ROOTS OF FRATERNAL ORGANIZATIONS and secret societies lie in the eighteenth century, but interest in the groups reached its peak one hundred years later. During the golden age of fraternalism, at the turn of the twentieth century, almost 40 percent of adult males were members of at least one fraternal organization. Although they were a global phenomenon, in the United States alone there were over one hundred thousand organizations, named after animals (Elks, Moose, Eagles), crusaders (Knights of Pythias, Knights of Columbus), professions (Masons, Foresters, Woodmen, Gleaners), and even their tendency to flout social expectations (Odd Fellows). Most of these organizations were founded to

1. do good in the community;
2. provide opportunities for professional networking or skill building;
3. offer financial benefits, such as life insurance;
4. provide a training ground for civic leadership; and
5. present a regular calendar of social events.

They were made up mostly of White men, although minorities founded their own orders or parallel organizations, and women often formed auxiliaries.

It is difficult to convey today how popular and integral to daily life fraternal organizations were during their heyday. In an age with restrictive social conventions and complicated (but unwritten) rules of conduct, a fraternal event offered the opportunity to enter a secret and permissive domain. One could escape standard conventions, dress in a costume, and engage in fantastic rituals with elaborate sets and props. In 1903 alone, more than one million Americans signed up to participate.

It was in this fertile environment that John W. Talbot crafted his own offering, the Order of Owls, in 1904. The Owls set as a major goal the enjoyment of life in the moment, or, as they put it, the "kingdom of heaven on earth." Talbot and the other founding members easily persuaded the wealthy and powerful to join, and growth was exponential. The Owls quickly became one of only a dozen or so organizations with membership over one hundred thousand, and at their peak they claimed nine hundred thousand members across the United States. For several decades after their founding, the Owls were mentioned in the top tier of social organizations.

To fund their operations and accomplish their charitable goals, fraternal organizations charged a range of fees and dues. Generally, there was an initial registration fee, which was split among the local chapter, the national body, and the organizer responsible for recruitment. Regular dues, which were again shared by the local and national organization, were paid weekly or monthly on an ongoing basis. To provide additional income, many organizations developed a broad range of branded merchandise. Members happily bought pins, scarves, swords, banners, and other regalia marked with the logos and mottoes of their particular group and displayed them with pride. The most successful organizations invested in real estate and built permanent offices and meeting halls. A 1904 report by the *Fraternal Monitor* (which did not include several of the largest organizations, such as the Masons, Odd Fellows, and Moose) valued the assets of America's fraternal organizations at almost $50 million.

Large amounts of money were coming in but also going out. Groups with an insurance function paid out for disability or death and paid maintenance to orphans and widows. They established hospitals and contributed to their communities in countless other ways. In 1900 these organizations were paying tens of millions (billions in today's dollars) annually in benefits. With so much money in play, the temptation to use this system for personal gain, for at least one man, was too much to resist.

ONE

—ɯ—

AN AUSPICIOUS BEGINNING

IT WAS A COLD NIGHT IN DECEMBER 1937 in South Bend, a bustling industrial town in northern Indiana. With Christmas only two weeks away, the day's newspaper was full of ads with suggestions for presents, and with no major stories to report, the Associated Press let the public know that department-store Santas were attempting to set a standard beard length. Early in the evening, as shoppers strolled past, smoke began to billow from the window of a downtown office building, followed by bright flames. The next day's paper would bear a banner headline with shocking news: "John W. Talbot Dies in Fire."[1] The same news was reported from coast to coast. Some mourned; more were relieved. But just who was John Talbot?

Owl motto from Owl letterhead, ca. 1910. *Letter privately held.*

Shortly after the end of the American Civil War, a brief but unusual birth announcement for John Talbot had appeared in a South Bend newspaper. The author wondered, "Who knows but that this new-comer may yet become President of the United States."[2]

John Joseph Talbot was born to Peter and Hannah Talbot (née Talbot) on December 12, 1869.[3] He was named for his maternal grandfather, and some sign must have motivated those who knew his family to predict a future of distinction. Although John would not become president, he would become powerful, influential, and famous, and he would count congressmen and senators among his friends.

The circumstances of his youth wouldn't seem to have marked him for greatness. John's father was a tailor who worked for the University of Notre Dame, and the family lived at 701 North Notre Dame Avenue, just a few blocks to the south of the university. The Talbots were among the first residents in the newly developed, largely Irish Catholic neighborhood. They worshipped on campus at Sacred Heart Church, and it was there that John was baptized.

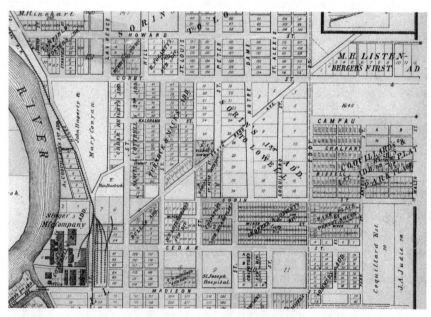

The Talbots owned lots 33 and 34 of Sorin's First Addition, seen at center. The Notre Dame campus is just out of view to the north. *Source:* Standard Atlas of St. Joseph County, Indiana (*Chicago: George A. Ogle, 1895*).

Typical homes in John's childhood neighborhood along Notre Dame
Avenue. Federal case file. *Source: National Archives, Chicago.*

In the Talbots' time, the university functioned very differently than it does
today, serving not just college students but boys as young as six.[4] Although
Notre Dame was founded by French Catholics, by midcentury the community
it served was mostly Irish. John's father, Peter, had attended Notre Dame as a
teenager, between 1856 and 1863, when there were only two hundred total students and the legendary Father Sorin was still president.[5] Peter was a manual
labor student, his parents paying a fifty-dollar entrance fee for their son to receive a basic education and be taught a trade.[6] His education was surprisingly
broad, including classes included in orthography and rhetoric, and he was even
in a play. After finishing school, Peter remained at the university working as a
tailor and was a resident there until his marriage.

Hannah was born in Ireland and came with her parents to South Bend at
the age of four along with two older sisters.[7] Hannah and Peter married in 1868.

Although John later would claim that he rose out of poverty, his family appeared financially secure and happy during his early childhood. His mother's
parents, John and Catherine Talbot, lived next door and were comfortably

middle-class. Hannah's father worked in the nearby Singer Sewing Machine factory as a foreman of the housekeeping crew. Both families were on firm financial footing, far from scraping by in fear of eviction. The 1870 census shows that both Peter Talbot and his in-laws owned their homes, valued then at $1,500 and $2,000, respectively ($30,000 and $40,000 in today's dollars).

John was four years old before there was another addition to the family, Joseph Edward Talbot, born November 26, 1873.[8] A sister, Mary Innocence, was born when John was seven but died in infancy in 1877.[9] After the birth of his brother, John's parents, perhaps to avoid confusion, seem to have changed John's middle name from Joseph to William, his father's middle name. Although John's family was small, the neighborhood was full of extended relatives. John's aunt Margaret (Talbot) Luther, with her large family, lived only a few doors away, and his great-aunt Johanna (Diggens) Clifford and her five children were within a few blocks. The Talbot, Luther, and Clifford families relied on each other, and John grew up surrounded by cousins close to his age.

The strong familial support structure was soon to be tested. Grandpa John died in 1874, and although he left a will and estate for the support of his widow, his presence must have been missed. More tragically, John's father, Peter, died at the age of forty-one in 1880, when John was only eleven. Again, provisions had been made: Peter left everything to his wife, who served as the executrix of his estate even though she was illiterate, as evidenced by her mark on the paperwork.[10] The family adopted a more frugal lifestyle, Hannah taking work as a seamstress, and her mother, Catherine, John's grandmother, moving in with them. John and Joseph were left with two strong women to raise them but no male role models in their immediate family, a deficit that would have consequences in their adult lives.

John began looking for ways to earn money to help out at home and later described some of these efforts, although his stories ring less than true. "In 1871 and 1872," he bragged, "I sold the first newspaper ever sold on the streets of South Bend."[11] Yet three local newspapers predated his childhood. One of these, the *Northwestern Pioneer*, was published forty years earlier, so it seems highly unlike that he pioneered newspaper sales "on the streets of South Bend." Not only that, but he would he have been just three years old as he stood on a corner hawking papers. What is certainly true is that from a young age John displayed an entrepreneurial spirit.

Undoubtedly, John relied on his network of relatives and neighborhood friends, which included future South Bend mayor E. J. Fogarty and notorious scoundrel "Colonel" Joseph Sullivan. Through Sullivan, who was known to jockey in illicit horse races, John became involved at a track only blocks from

Portrait of John's brother, Joseph, taken while a student at Notre Dame. *Photo courtesy of the University of Notre Dame Archives.*

his house. He later noted that one of the major newspaper editors liked to insult him by calling him a "race horse tout," someone who spies on racehorses in training to gain information for betting.[12] John would have been paid for the service. Sullivan would become a popular and successful Irish saloon owner and gambler and John's lifelong friend. Together, John and Sullivan learned how to take advantage of the gullible to make easy money.

John also claimed to have dabbled in more respectable work. He reported that he took a job in a store run by a woman he called Old Maid Ryan, working as "a cashboy employed at 50 cents a week."[13] He was not a good employee: "No doubt, I was pretty objectionable, and the old girl discharged me."[14] He would later credit this experience with giving him the push he needed to leave a job with no future and go on to have a successful career. "Many a person can afford to be thankful for some Old Maid Ryan who forced him to take a ship by kicking him from a water-logged plank of which he was afraid to let go."

John's mother was determined to give the boys an education and fed their ambition to rise above a working-class life. Both John and Joseph attended Notre Dame like their father, but not as manual labor students. As day students (residing off campus), they completed the commercial course, a two-year program that required basic math, reading, and writing skills and offered a number of other courses, including geography and history. Joseph took drawing, while John took bookkeeping and rhetoric, skills he would certainly put to use. John received his diploma in 1886, at the age of seventeen. Joseph followed in 1890. Although the brothers would claim that Joseph returned to Notre Dame for a law degree, in fact he went back at the college level in 1896 but stayed only one semester.[15] Unfortunately, as John was reaching adulthood, another anchor in his life was preparing to let go. His grandmother, sensing her health failing, made out a will in 1886, splitting her property equally between her two surviving daughters.[16] She named Judge Timothy Howard, a fellow Irishman and family friend, as the executor of her estate. She died on July 19, 1892, at the age of seventy-five.

With his grandmother declining, there must have been pressure on Talbot to establish himself in the world. John had close relatives in Detroit, and going there was seen as a great opportunity to get a start as an attorney by "training in one of the finest law offices in the city."[17] As a young man, he had already mastered the use of hyperbole.

The process of becoming an attorney was very different in 1890 from what it is today. The standardized bar exam that is now the terror of so many law students had yet to be developed. Michigan did not establish a state board of bar examiners until 1895.[18] Prior to that, the procedure for admission to the bar was by examination by the court.[19] They were looking for "good moral character"[20] and "sufficient legal learning and ability to discharge the duties of such office."[21] After passing this oral exam, Talbot would simply have been asked to take an oath and pay a fee.

Although city directories never show him as a Detroit resident, newspapers report he was admitted to practice in 1892.[22] He worked out of the McGraw building, which was full of professionals: lawyers, insurance agents, and real estate men.[23] During this time the Detroit College of Law[24] was founded and operated not only out of the same building but the same office where Talbot worked, though there is no record that he had any connection to the school

The McGraw Building, Detroit, ca. 1920. Talbot worked out of room 20.
Photo courtesy of the Detroit Public Library.

as either a student or a founder. There is evidence that his activities weren't confined to the study of law. A small classified ad listing John W. Talbot as a contact offered "Lot on Locust. Easy Terms." Clearly, Talbot was also gaining basic skills in the manipulation of real estate.[25]

Talbot's time in Detroit formed him as a professional and brought two other important things into his life: a wife and venture capital. While in Detroit, John met Mary "Minnie" O'Brien, a young Irish woman described as "an accomplished and most highly esteemed young lady."[26] Her father, Patrick, had overcome the limitations of a spinal disease contracted in the Civil War to create a thriving retail business. By the time the condition finally killed him in 1880, he left an estate worth $20,000. The match was exceedingly fortuitous for John. Whether for love or money, John married Minnie in Detroit's Holy Trinity Church on September 24, 1895.[27] John was twenty-six, Minnie twenty-seven.

Undoubtedly, Minnie brought to the marriage enough money to give the couple a healthy start back in South Bend. John promptly moved his wife into a grand, newly built house at 729 East Cedar Street, on the corner of St. Peter and Cedar, opposite the St. Joseph Hospital and a few blocks from his mother and brother. On December 8, 1896, just over a year after they were married, Minnie Talbot delivered a son. He was named John Harold Talbot, after his father.[28]

At twenty-seven, John had overcome the obstacles of his childhood using intelligence and tenacity. He had learned from his family and friends that loyalty was more important than honesty and that finding a sucker was a quick way to make money. Old Maid Ryan had taught him to think of what others would call a work ethic as weakness, that the truly successful get others to do the work for them. Now he would put these lessons to use. He had a family, a fine house, and money in his pocket, and he was determined to take on the world.

TWO

—∽—

A BUDDING CAREER AND
A BLOSSOMING CRIMINAL

JOHN BEGAN PRACTICING LAW just after his marriage, setting up his South Bend firm with a partner as Talbot & Horne. Fifteen years John's senior, Albert J. Horne had trained in the law under noted local judge (and Talbot family friend) Timothy Howard but had set up a legal practice only a few years before John was admitted to the bar. Horne was primarily known as a property developer and had a clear influence on John's interest in real estate. Between 1893 and 1896, the two Talbot brothers were involved in twenty land transactions. They purchased and sold land for profit but just as often appeared in cases where there seemed to be a need to clear a title. Clients would sell property to the Talbots for one dollar as a quitclaim, which includes no protection for the buyer. The Talbots would immediately sell it back as a warranty deed, guaranteeing that the title was unencumbered. They often used this tactic when a divorcing couple who had held property in common was transferring the property to just one spouse.

Talbot & Horne initially occupied a small office at 115 North Main in South Bend, but after John purchased a three-story building across the street on the prominent corner of Colfax and Main, the partnership moved to that more prestigious location. What would become known as the Talbot Building at 138 North Main would anchor John's activities for the next three decades.

John's brother, Joseph, initially had no intention of following his brother into law. He had been training as a machinist at Sibley & Ware, a large concern only a few blocks from the family home. However, John had higher aspirations for Joseph (if Joseph didn't have them for himself). John convinced Joseph to abandon that trade and train as a lawyer under him. As soon as Joseph was old enough, John rebranded his law office "Talbot & Talbot," and Horne left to pursue his own interests. The Talbot brothers' business consisted mainly of divorces and criminal defense, and their services were widely sought after. John was described as a "hustling, wide-awake young attorney of this city, who has a growing practice and the ability to take care of it."[1] Yet allegations of misconduct came quickly. In 1897 John was indicted for the receipt of stolen property: a carload (1,600 yards) of silk from the B & O Railroad. "The goods in question consist of a large quantity of silks which last September were thrown from a Baltimore and Ohio freight car near Walkerton, this county [St. Joseph]. The silks found their way to a hayloft near here, and later to room 11, Hotel Columbia, this city [South Bend], where on Saturday night officers seized them."[2] Authorities were on the lookout for the missing fabric, and Talbot had raised suspicions by sending a large shipment to Chicago to be dyed.[3] During the subsequent investigation, the sheriff located Kate McCollum, a woman whom John allegedly set up as a broker to sell the silk after it was processed, and John was charged in court with grand larceny. With silk selling between seventy cents and a dollar a yard, the illicit sale would bring in several times more than most men earned in a year.[4]

The case should have been cut and dried, but John was determined to put up a fight. He succeeded in getting the venue changed from St. Joseph to Marshall County, the next county to the south. It was a tactic he would employ again and again in the coming years, usually because he was confident he could influence the judge or jury in the new location. John kept the focus of the proceedings not on whether or not he was guilty but on the technical details of the prosecution. He challenged every fact presented, including whether prosecutors could prove the crime took place in the county where the case had been brought. Despite strong evidence, after six days of testimony the jury took only thirteen minutes to acquit Talbot on a technicality.[5]

Although John escaped unscathed, a casualty of the trial was Talbot's relationship with Albert Horne. Horne had been subpoenaed to testify, and John allegedly attempted to blackmail him into staying silent. When Horne didn't comply, the details of an earlier sordid case, supposedly kept quiet by Horne, were somehow suddenly exposed to the public. As Horne was widely respected in the community, the Talbots were unable to do permanent damage to his reputation, but these events began to paint a portrait of John as calculating, corrupt, and vengeful.[6]

The silk case notwithstanding, John's criminal defense practice wasn't established to defend himself. It included soon-to-be-high-profile clients. During this period, the notorious Lake Shore Gang was running rampant across

CASE AGAINST TALBOT FAILED.

An Attorney Charged With Receiving Stolen Goods is Acquitted.

From the *Bremen (IN) Enquirer*, January 18, 1898.

northern Indiana and Ohio. Train robbers named for the Lake Shore and Michigan Southern Railroad, the gang robbed passengers and often stole the contents of the train cars (it was believed that the gang was the source of the silk that ended up in Talbot's possession, perhaps as payment for his services).[7] They also committed bank robberies and residential break-ins along the route, using the train as a means of escape. In arresting John, law enforcement officials had hoped they would be able to break the gang. "The police claim that they may now be able to unravel a gigantic scheme to rob railroads in which it is intimated some prominent people are concerned. The principal sufferers are the Baltimore & Ohio and Lake Shore, which roads have been robbed frequently for months. Underwear, overcoats and shoes were brought in today by the police, and more goods are to come."[8] However, John refused to speak against the gang and after he was acquitted continued to act as their attorney.

The frequency and boldness of the Lake Shore Gang's activities was creating anxiety among the public, as reflected in a report from Goshen, Indiana:

> Goshen is suffering from an epidemic of holdups and burglaries. There has been no night in two weeks without an attempt to enter some home. The local police officers seem powerless to grapple with the situation, and the people are becoming alarmed. While waiting at the Lake Shore Station for a train, in a spot much frequented and within four blocks of the courthouse, B. B. Bortner, a civil engineer, was robbed. The thieves, not satisfied with taking his money, appropriated his shoes and hat.... Some of the officers fear ... the Lake Shore Gang ... is at the bottom of the trouble.[9]

Fear of the gang was so pervasive that almost any crime, large or small, that took place in the Midwest in the 1890s was attributed to the Lake Shore Gang. In Minnesota the gang was considered responsible for robbing migrant workers.

The Lake Shore Gang's hideout as it looks today, a ravine between
the cities of South Bend and Mishawaka. *Photo by the author.*

"Hobos up and down the line stand in terror of the gang, who are believed
to be part of the famous Lake Shore Gang from Chicago, who annually visit
this section to pluck the luckless woodsman or harvest hand."[10] In Cleveland
they were accused of boldly robbing a patrolman of "his money, watch, 'billy,'
revolver, and a pair of handcuffs."[11] In Elyria, Ohio, the newspaper defended
the community's palpable concerns: "The inference drawn that members of the
notorious Lake Shore Gang are responsible for many of the recent robberies
and brutal attacks upon the unwary is entirely justifiable."[12] The sheer volume
of criminal activity blamed on the gang became remarkable and unlikely. One
article in a Michigan newspaper claimed that "the records in the post office
department will show hundreds of post office robberies in Ohio, Michigan, and
Indiana, and some in Illinois. Nearly all the bank robberies and safe blowings
in these states within a hundred miles of the Lake Shore railway can be traced
to members of this desperate gang of thieves."[13] Membership in the Lake Shore
Gang was speculated to be in the hundreds, and their hideout was reported to
be a ravine near the railroad tracks on the fringes of South Bend.

The main players in the Lake Shore Gang's Richland, Michigan, court drama. *Source:* South Bend (IN) Tribune, *May 6, 1899.*

On August 5, 1898, the gang was credited with a bold daytime bank robbery in Richland, Michigan. Nitroglycerine charges were used to blow off the front of the building, and the gang threatened to kill citizens who came to investigate the noise. Despite being surrounded by a crowd of shocked onlookers, the criminals made their escape with about $50,000 worth of coins, paper money, and bonds. However, their notoriety and the large number of witnesses made it hard for the perpetrators to hide. A few months later, authorities began catching up with members of the gang, and the leaders, "Yock" Allison and Harry Slater, were put on trial in Kalamazoo, Michigan, in May 1899. Their attorneys? None other than John and Joseph Talbot.

It is notable that only a few weeks after the robbery, the Talbot brothers appear to have come into a substantial amount of money. They used it to purchase a large tract of land, which they promptly subdivided and offered for sale, naming one of the newly formed streets Talbot Avenue.[14] Two of the first purchases were registered to Harry Foote and John Jennings, which were aliases for the gang leaders. Foote and Jennings paid for the land with gold.

As the gang members went on trial, Joseph attended the proceedings in the courtroom, while John (allegedly) collected false depositions and fabricated evidence. During testimony, there were allusions to the possibility that Joseph was tampering with witnesses, although at least one denied this on the stand.[15] John contacted his closest associates, including John Johnson, who shared his office, and assembled a ledger purported to be from the Columbia Hotel in a remote city the night before the robbery. It showed that Allison and Slater had stayed with Johnson and, if true, proved they could not have committed the crime. Unfortunately, the ledger was not John's best work: "A little examination showed that there had been some fixing of that book to get it in shape to be of use. The date slip, August 4, was raised and beneath it was another, September 1. The last page in the book had been cut out, and several shifts in the pages made, all of which were bungling. . . . The alibi for the defendants is knocked completely out. . . . There may be some perjury prosecutions."[16]

Allison and Slater were found guilty, sentenced to seventeen years, and sent to the state penitentiary in Jackson, Michigan. Immediately, questions arose concerning the laxity of their treatment, which the Talbots almost certainly had a hand in arranging. Despite his status as a leader of the "notorious" and "bloody" Lake Shore Gang, Slater was granted the status of trusty, giving him broad privileges and freedom of movement. It was this freedom that allowed Allison, Slater, and others to escape the prison in August 1904.[17] The assumption was that they were headed back to South Bend, one newspaper stating, "The bank robbers are on their way to Indiana."[18]

They were simply heading home. Earlier, a newspaper had noted, "The principal hang out is in South Bend, where the lawyers for the gang reside.... They have two of the smartest lawyers in Indiana to get them out of trouble and these lawyers have grown rich, prosperous, and influential out of the gang."[19] They had women they knew would shelter them, and the Talbots allegedly gave them food, clothing, and money and arranged for transportation and housing as the convicts made their way south. One report even claimed that John Talbot had personally arranged the details of their escape and that Joseph Talbot had provided Allison with one of his own suits to replace his prison uniform.[20] Eventually, the escaped convicts would be rounded up or killed as they ran from authorities. None of the gang ultimately evaded justice, except the Talbots themselves.

Criminal defense was not John's only pursuit during this time. He was also making the rounds as a guest speaker, holding forth at a Democratic meeting in June 1900 and addressing another crowd on the Fourth of July. "At two o'clock, John W. Talbot, of South Bend, delivered an interesting address in the grove near town and had the attention of a large audience. Mr. Talbot is a very forcible speaker and handled his address with much credit."[21] John was racking up public speaking experience and name recognition, further developing his personal clout.

Talbot again made headlines for executing an unusual marriage contract that demonstrated his willingness to ignore societal norms. For some unspecified reason, a young couple from southern Michigan wanted to wed without the involvement of a minister or justice of the peace. Rather than vowing "till death do us part," John Hanover and Berta Best signed Talbot's contract saying, "The party of the second part ... does take the party of the first part for her husband from the time of the execution of this contract until the death of one of the said parties."[22]

By 1900, John and Joseph were wealthy, well known, and powerful. They were also solidly tied to organized crime and had recently defended the most notorious criminals in the region. The next logical step in their careers? Politics. They moved to position Joseph to win the office of state prosecuting attorney for the county. The primary function of this office is to act as the state's agent to prosecute criminals charged with committing crimes in their district. If successful, Joseph would, on paper, become the instant enemy of those he had so recently been defending.

With no indication of irony, Joseph campaigned hard to gain the office. Despite his professional past, citizens saw him as "an able and painstaking practitioner [who] possesses all the essentials for a successful and prosperous

JOSEPH E. TALBOT

IS A GOOD LAWYER   A GOOD CITIZEN
A TAX PAYER

You want a good lawyer for prosecuting attorney because only a lawyer having the ability can represent your interests in the enforcement of the law.

You want a good citizen and taxpayer in this office because he is interested as much as you in protecting you and your rights.

As far as this office is concerned the question of party is not of importance as is the character and the legal ability of the candidate.

You will be voting for your own interest if you vote for

JOSEPH E. TALBOT.

One of many large newspaper ads placed by Joseph Talbot in the run-up to the election. *Source:* South Bend (IN) Tribune, *November 3, 1906.*

career."[23] In 1900 Joseph wrote the president of the University of Notre Dame, the Reverend Andrew Morrissey, to solicit support for his campaign. He noted that he was "practically assured of the nomination." He admitted that until that time he had been mainly engaged in criminal defense but said he would abandon that work if elected. He further stated, "I pledge you the conferring of any favors at my behest consistent with the performance of my duty."[24] Although he didn't yet hold the office, he was already promising favors in exchange for support.

Joseph's first campaign was unsuccessful. He didn't even receive the nomination to the ticket (the spot going to a business partner of the Talbots, Francis Jackson—still a win for John). But the Talbots were persistent. In the 1906 election, Joseph took out a full-page ad in the *South Bend Tribune* that included an endorsement from Timothy Howard, the respected local judge. No other candidate, even those for Congress, had advertising on that scale. The last line read, "You will be voting for your own interest if you vote for Joseph E. Talbot."[25] In fact, after winning the election he would immediately begin to serve his own interests.

Those interests included his own growing family. Joseph married Edith Thompson on July 5, 1904.[26] The couple moved to 624 North Notre Dame Avenue, directly across from his mother, less than a block away from John, and a block from the house he grew up in. Joseph and Edith had two children, Dorothy in 1906 and Joseph Jr. in 1909.

Meanwhile, in addition to running his thriving legal practice, John was, according to one witness, embroiled in a broad range of nefarious activity. Criminal defense attorneys are compelled to associate with the worst elements of society, but Talbot crossed the line with his involvement. His name was linked to three major gangs, his role not strictly limited to representing them in court. One former associate stated, "He is the center, the brains and the controlling spirit of the biggest gang of thieves, robbers, cut-throats, blackmailers and buncosteerers that have ever preyed upon the people" and connected him to the swindler "Red" Austin, a member of the Gold Brick Gang.[27] Named for a scam that convinced an unsuspecting bystander to pay $5,000 for what was, in fact, a clay brick painted gold, the gang operated throughout the Midwest.

John was also implicated in the activities of the Maybray Gang. Led by John C. Maybray, the group of expert swindlers perpetrated crimes nationwide. "The Maybray gang . . . stole more than $2,000,000 before the doors of the prison opened for it. . . . The devices of the Maybray gang . . . were fake foot races, fake wrestling matches, fake prize fights, fake horse races, fake poolrooms, and all the host of iniquitous schemes used to separate the covetous from their money."[28] In addition to staging sporting events, they developed a device that appeared to print money, which they sold to naive victims for over $1,000.

One scam in South Bend involved William J. Springborn, the chairman of the Board of Public Works in Cleveland. The gang lured him to South Bend with the promise of a land deal, persuading him not only to bring along a large amount of cash but also to attend a wrestling match while he was in town—and to bet $300, all he could draw on his bank, on the outcome. Unknown to Springborn, all the other participants, wrestlers and bystanders alike, were in on the swindle. His was the only money on the line. With a gang member holding Springborn's $300, plus $10,000 for the land, the match commenced. Soon after it started, one of the wrestlers pretended to be seriously hurt, perhaps mortally, and Springborn was hurried away and onto a train leaving town to keep his name out of the scandal that would surely ensue. In the rush, his money was left in the hands of the organizer. That might have been the end of it but for the fact that while looking out the window of his train as it passed the site of the match, Springborn saw his former associates sharing out his money among themselves. He made his way back to town and had the group hauled in by authorities. John,

Frank Webb was caught while trying to break members of the Lake Shore Gang out of jail in Kalamazoo, Michigan. Alleged to be working for Talbot, he was frequently in trouble with the law. He died in prison in Michigan City, Indiana. *Source: Indiana State Archives, Indianapolis.*

never far from the action, was present at the scene and stepped in on behalf of the "hurt" wrestler, a local boy, causing enough of a diversion to slip his client out the back, leaving the rest of the gang to face prosecution.[29]

When post offices were robbed in Chicago and South Bend, a witness claimed John was involved. "It was John W. Talbot who ... when I was about to enter his private office, told me not to do so, saying that [Frank] Webb (the man who recently went to the penitentiary for killing the sheriff of Pulaski county) and the boys are in there counting stamps. And John told me not to look in there or they might blow my d——d head off." Talbot, the witness said, "showed me a big roll of postage stamps and said they were worth $1,800 and told me they came easy.... That was after the big robbery of the Chicago post office and before the stamp thieves visited the South Bend post office—plenty of time ... to run out of stamps."[30]

John Talbot was dynamic and successful, and his reputation was at this point remarkably untarnished, despite his questionable associates. Although this would change soon enough, for a time the young attorney was free to devote his remarkable energy to his legal practice, his social life, and a variety of entrepreneurial enterprises.

THREE

—ᴍ—

DIVERSIFICATION

Social Networks, Political Influence, and the Importance of Family

JOHN MAY HAVE LOST HIS FATHER and grandfather early on, but he grew up surrounded by aunts, uncles, and cousins in a tight-knit community. There was an expectation that they would all care for and support one another, and as a young man John had the chance to prove his loyalty to his family.

Just after John's marriage, his great-uncle Dennis Clifford passed away. Although Dennis had several adult children, one of Dennis's sons had predeceased him, so his death left four grandchildren who had previously relied on him with no support. The family respected John's legal expertise and real estate experience, so even though the oldest of these children were only a few years younger than John, he was awarded guardianship of his cousins.

John provided legal services for the estate and managed the sale of several parcels of real estate that had belonged to his great-uncle. The sales yielded about $200 for each child (about $6,000 today). The oldest child, Margaret, promptly married. Because the next two, Estelle and Dennis, were already living on their own, John managed their assets and distributed the money to them when they reached the age of twenty-one. However, the youngest, Jeremiah, was only fifteen when his grandfather died. With John's wife, Minnie, pregnant with their first child, it would have been awkward for John to take in Jeremiah to raise as his own. Instead, Jeremiah was housed with his uncle Patrick (another of John's cousins), who had lost his only child in a tragic accident. John managed Jeremiah's money, regularly providing him with clothes, schoolbooks, a watch, and other necessities and declining to charge the customary fees because of his "blood relation" to the boy. Once the boy reached maturity, John turned over his assets to him, as he had for his other cousins.[1] Since many of John's later

Edward J. Fogarty, mayor of South Bend, was John's age and grew up two houses from the Talbot family. *Source:* South Bend— World Famed (*South Bend: South Bend Central Labor Union, 1909*).

business dealings were questionable, it is tempting to wonder whether he took advantage of these vulnerable minors. Yet John's handling of his obligations to his cousins seems to have been completely above board.

By all accounts, John was a busy young man. He was raising a family, his law practice was thriving, and he had begun dabbling in real estate: offering homes for rent, buying and selling property, and acquiring a significant portfolio. He quietly developed a stake in concerns such as the Mishawaka Realty Company and South Bend White Coal. His cousins and friends had been busy, too. They began with jobs in the trades, as masons, carpenters, and plumbers. Soon the family found their way into politics, initially as Democrats. By 1900 the Talbots, Luthers, Cliffords, and their friends formed an East Side Democratic machine that would come to dominate politics in the city for two decades. In 1901 the Talbots' childhood friend and next-door neighbor, Edward J. Fogarty, ran for

The *South Bend Tribune* ran daily cartoons depicting the Fogarty administration as corrupt. *Source:* South Bend (IN) Tribune, *November 6, 1905.*

mayor of South Bend, with John's cousin, Patrick Clifford, described as his "principal advisor."[2] Fogarty won and quickly rewarded those who had helped him gain the position with patronage positions in public works, public safety, and the post office.

Fogarty successfully ran for reelection three times. In every cycle the opposition, using the Republican-leaning *South Bend Tribune* as a vehicle, vehemently characterized his administration as deeply corrupt. For weeks prior to the elections, the front page ran editorials and cartoons describing Fogarty's "City Hall Clique," "vice ring," and "gang" and showing Fogarty and his inner circle personally profiting from the taxpayers. The cartoons in particular bothered Joseph Talbot (himself running for office), who repeatedly delivered speeches calling for them to cease. Not surprisingly, the local Democratic paper

Patrick Clifford, John's
cousin. *Source:* Pictorial
Souvenir of South Bend,
Indiana *(South Bend, IN:
J. J. McVicker, 1919).*

painted a very different picture. The *South Bend News-Times* depicted Fogarty
as a man who got things done, a man of progressive ideas who pushed improvements, a man friendly to business who helped the city grow.[3]

The 1905 election was particularly bitter. During political meetings, nails
were driven into car tires and gas tanks drained. Attempts were made to cut
the electrical wires to the meeting sites. The day of the election there were reports of intoxicated election officials at polling sites, and the police were called
to multiple locations to investigate. It was understatedly hailed as "the most
spirited [campaign] in many years."[4]

Fogarty ultimately served four terms, during which the extended Talbot
family profited greatly and consolidated their influence. Later, not standing on
principle, the family would turn away from a Democratic mayoral candidate

Left, James Luther, John's cousin. *Source:* Pictorial Souvenir of South Bend, Indiana (*South Bend, IN: J. J. McVicker, 1919*).

Right, Joseph Luther, John's cousin. *Source:* South Bend (IN) Tribune, *December 18, 1924.*

promising to clean up the city, and work to elect a Republican, Frank Carson, who was friendlier to their interests and just as willing to award them lucrative positions.

Initially rewarded with a mail carrier's route, cousin Patrick Clifford came to be described as a "dictator" in the Democratic Party in South Bend.[5] Cousin James Luther, originally a milkman, was made superintendent of the water works under Carson and would eventually hold positions as county commissioner and Fourth Ward councilman; he also sat on the city's Board of Safety and its Alcoholic Beverage Commission. Trained as a plumber, cousin Joseph Luther received a position in the police department under Mayor Fogarty, and "his political influence increased to unusual proportions."[6] He eventually served as a city meter inspector, and chief doorkeeper of the state legislature.

Joe Sullivan, John's lifelong friend. *Source: Charles S. Beckley,* South Bend Phizes and Pointers *(South Bend, IN: printed by author, ca. 1912).*

Under both Fogarty and Carson, and with a state's attorney turning a blind eye, vice ran rampant in the city, to the benefit of the Talbots and their friends. The *Tribune* expressed outrage and tried to organize resistance: "A movement to compel Mayor Fogarty to cease permitting evil to be flaunted in the face of the public is under consideration," an attempt to mitigate the prevailing "outrageous moral conditions."[7]

John Talbot seemed very happy with these conditions, as were his associates. His old friend Joe Sullivan was making a fortune selling wholesale liquor and running gambling schemes, along with a little legitimate business.

Another boy from the neighborhood, William McInerny, ran a successful tobacco shop and billiard room. The Talbots themselves were reputed to be involved in gambling and prostitution at a spot at 121 West Colfax Avenue, opposite their offices, in an area described as the "tenderloin district" of South Bend (a few doors from City Hall, hardly an out-of-the-way corner).[8] They reportedly partnered with a local madame, Madge Cole, who was repeatedly arrested for operating a house of ill repute and charged with running a gambling and liquor joint. With no police pressure, these businesses boomed, but public scrutiny eventually forced Cole out of the Colfax building. She relocated to 1521 West Washington, just outside the city limits. Her partner was Joseph Sullivan.

John undoubtedly benefited from his strengthening connections to people of influence, but he himself never ran for office or took a public service position. Why? Because these men were blue collar, and Talbot was a professional. John's vision was bigger, his sights set higher. John's eye saw far beyond a small town in the Midwest and even beyond the state. His dreams were of a national stage. From boyhood, John worked to develop a very particular set of skills, such as how to manipulate people to get what he wanted, motivating some and threatening others. He practiced his public speaking and honed his written arguments. He hardened to using tactics others saw as extreme. He learned these new skills quickly and deployed them rapidly to advance his personal agenda.

John and Joseph were clearly anxious to move up in the world, and a social organization presented an opportunity to network with other professionals and gain prominence. As Catholics, the Talbot brothers were barred from many fraternal organizations, but there was one major exception, the Hibernians. South Bend's Irish Catholics had organized a local chapter of the Ancient Order of Hibernians on January 11, 1885. Although the Talbots were not old enough to be among the charter members, they became involved and moved up the ranks as soon as they were able. In 1895, as his legal practice was just getting off the ground, the twenty-six-year-old John W. Talbot is listed as vice president of the organization. Joseph was also heavily involved but did not hold office.

The Hibernians' goal was to promote friendship, unity, and Christian charity.[9] In 1901 John was one of the featured speakers at a Hibernian event, lecturing on the topic of Sir Thomas More, the sixteenth-century English Catholic philosopher, statesman, and author.[10] It was an interesting choice for Talbot, considering that in More's *Utopia* he abolishes the legal profession.

As time went on, John's involvement with the Hibernians dwindled. Perhaps there were too many demands on John's time, but John's faith (or lack of it) may also have been an issue. His status as a "good Catholic" was in question by the time he founded a new fraternal organization in 1904, which put him at odds with the Hibernians, who were heavily tied to the Church. Ultimately, John would become an atheist. Joseph, on the other hand, remained a practicing Catholic throughout his life.[11]

A history of the Hibernians makes a point of stating that "all were men of good moral character with high ideals of morality and citizenship. . . . It was very rare that anyone with a known undesirable habit applied for membership."[12] John Talbot's undesirable habits were not yet widely known.

John's professional success masked problems on the home front. Soon after the birth of their son, Minnie started spending more and more time away from home. She was back in Detroit with her family long enough that the 1900 census indicated that she lived there and a newspaper article mentioned that "Talbot's wife is said to live in Detroit."[13] It is possible that the two were ill-suited for one another from the beginning. Regardless, it is clear that John devoted most of his energy to his work and interests, not his home and family. Minnie's absences allowed John to explore a string of relationships with other women. At least three of Talbot's lovers made statements that Mrs. Talbot was out of town for extended periods, which they knew from spending time at her house. If Minnie knew of these affairs (and it is likely she did), she doesn't appear to have fought for her man. Instead, she devoted her life to raising her son, leaving John the time and space to pursue new opportunities.

THE FOUNDING OF THE ORDER OF OWLS

THE TURN OF THE TWENTIETH CENTURY was the golden age of the fraternal organization, and many men (and women) belonged to one or more groups. By the late 1800s, there were organizations with long histories, such as the Masons and the Odd Fellows; animal-inspired groups like the Moose, Eagles, and Elks; and esoteric associations like the Woodmen of the World. Some operated on a theme, such as the Improved Order of Red Men, who dressed as "Indians" and drew their inspiration from the Sons of Liberty and the Boston Tea Party. What they all had in common was that they offered a social outlet and networking opportunities and espoused generally charitable goals. Many organizations offered a form of death and disability insurance or other hardship benefit to members. Most were exclusively White. Some offered parallel organizations for African Americans, although exclusively Black groups, such as the United Brothers of Friendship, formed as well.

John Talbot had experience as a member of the Ancient Order of Hibernians, and he would have known the myriad other organizations represented in South Bend: Masons, Elks, and so on. However, as a Catholic, Talbot was not allowed to join some of these groups. The Talbot brothers wanted to expand their influence. They wanted access to the upper tiers of society and to men with power, and they wanted to make easy money. The Talbots and their friends decided that creating their own organization would meet all of these goals, and they immediately set out to do so.

Fraternal organizations are often dedicated in principle to specific charitable causes or generally doing good in the world. In contrast, this new organization would be devoted to "love, laughter, and the kingdom of heaven on earth"—in other words, the enjoyment of life in the moment. And what to call themselves? There was a popular establishment John was known to frequent called the Owl Saloon, located in the alley behind his office (then called Center Street). Is it coincidental that the organization that was to rise to prominence took its name from this rough liquor joint just steps from Talbot's place of business? Was it inside the Owl, in fact, that Talbot and his friends debated the merits and shortcomings of existing fraternal organizations and determined to launch their own? Whatever the case, on November 20, 1904, the Order of Owls was born. John's written description of its creation took this form,

> A few fellows—good fellows—got together, had a talk. Then a few other fellows—good fellows—joined them. That was in South Bend. There were Jno. W. Talbot, wit, lecturer, lawyer; Geo. Beroth, whose ears have a knack of turning to fellows with trouble. J. Lott Losey was one of them, and Frank Dunbar, who said, "Good fellows always die." It's proved—he's dead. J. W. Hill, celebrated as physician and philosopher, joined the company, and there were others. They were the nucleus. There was no attempt to build a society. This great modern fraternity was not made or organized. It happened— came about. It was the result of the attraction of fellows by other fellows, a force that has made many lodges and has members in all the states. That's the Order of Owls.[1]

John Talbot's claim that there was no effort given to the creation of the Owls was untrue. He did his homework. He traveled across the country to fraternal conventions, learning about the structure and methods of other organizations. John and his brother, Joseph, wrote a constitution and bylaws, which John later modestly called "the fruit of months of work of the best constitutional lawyers in the Middle West."[2] He borrowed liberally from the Independent International Order of Owls, a Masonic branch founded fifteen years earlier, open only to Master Masons. These Owls assigned their leaders the title of "supreme," which caught Talbot's fancy, as did the Masonic Owls' use of "nests" to name local chapters. Although the older order, backed by the power of the Masons, could have stopped Talbot's fledgling organization, there is no evidence they tried. When Talbot launched his own Owls, there were only about twenty-five hundred Masonic Owls in total nationwide, a number Talbot was quickly on pace to equal and surpass. It seems the Masons preferred to devote their resources to other aspects of their organization.

John was installed as president, or "Supreme Owl," and Joseph would serve as the Owl attorney. The other founding members were George D. Beroth, supreme secretary; J. Lott Losey, supreme treasurer; and John J. Johnson, John D. Burke, William Weaver, and Frank Dunbar. They adopted a motto:

> There's so much bad in the best of us
> And so much good in the worst of us
> It hardly behooves any of us
> To speak ill of the rest of us[3]

Interestingly, many of the Talbot brothers' usual associates, most notably his Clifford and Luther cousins, and friends Joe Sullivan and William McInerny, were not included in this new enterprise.

The constitution laid out the organization's goals: "to assist each other in business, to help each other in obtaining employment, to assist the widows and orphans of our brothers, to give aid to our brothers in any way that they may need, and assemble for mutual pleasure and entertainment." They also stated that they would "respect the honor of our women." This last goal would prove to be a struggle for John personally, but he had little to fear in terms of repercussions for misconduct. The constitution he had written made it nearly impossible for the Supreme Owl to be removed from his position. Membership requirements were simple. At first, any White man of any religious denomination over the age of sixteen could join. Later, "ladies' nests" were formed as well. Meetings were generally held once a week.

As far as Owl finances were concerned, it was highly publicized that officers would not receive salaries, and article 1 of the organization states clearly, "The Order shall never be conducted for profit or as a business enterprise."[4] Those interested in joining bought into their initial membership, usually for around five dollars, although most advertising warned that the cost would be much higher when the charter was "closed."[5] This up-front money was split between the organizer responsible for bringing in the prospective member and the local nest. Organizations relied on local men willing to spend time and energy drumming up interest and getting people to join their club as opposed to someone else's. Organizing was a potentially lucrative occupation, and Talbot published an appeal that was anything but subtle: "Be an Owl organizer and get rich."[6] Given the presence of two attorneys and the money involved, it is interesting to note that John filed no official articles of association or incorporation, either at the time of the formation of the order or in the years thereafter.[7]

Members paid fifty cents in monthly dues, of which ten cents quarterly went back to the home nest in South Bend. This was consistent with the

CATALOGUE

of

Lodge Equipment
Aids to Initiation
Advertising Novelties
Jewelry, Emblems
Prizes, Etc., Etc.

S▬▬ Sold by the

OWL ▬▬▬▬ DEPARTMENT

Home Nest Order of Owls

OWL BUILDING
HARTFORD, CON▬

Cover of the Owl *Catalogue of Lodge Equipment, Aids to Initiation, Advertising Novelties, Jewelry, Emblems, Prizes, Etc., Etc.* (South Bend, IN: Home Nest Order of Owls, ca. 1910).

requirements of other fraternal organizations. The question became how the home nest would use this money. As Talbot publicly laid out, the money collected was earmarked for charitable work and member assistance. In fact, very little of the funds would be used in that way, a deviation made possible by the lack of accountability for organizations in this period: "Most groups were neither regulated nor followed any established accounting procedures, opening them to embezzlement and fraud."[8] Although many clubs were vulnerable to unscrupulous actors, it is probable that the Owl founders intended from the beginning to defraud the membership. Certainly, over the next two decades John and Joseph Talbot and likely the rest of the Owl officers would use the money collected from members for personal gain and to fund extravagant lifestyles, leaving very little in the Owl bank account.

In thinking through the details of their club, the Owl founders were extremely thorough. They wanted this young organization to have the feel of a much more established one, with the side benefit of reaping profits from the sale of Owl-themed merchandise. At an early meeting someone brought back from Chicago a trio of taxidermized owls on a branch, and the enduring logo of the Owls was born. With the help of J. Lott Losey, a founding member and jeweler by trade, the founders designed an organizational structure and all the associated paraphernalia: ribbons, buttons, robes, letterhead, and so on, all available for purchase in a glossy catalog. One could even buy an Owl suit, for "much hilarity and clean, innocent fun can be added to the ceremony of initiation of new members by proper costuming."[9] Talbot's macabre sense of humor is evident in some of the products: "The emblem of the second degree is a large gold disc surmounted by a skull. On the disc appears a coffin and on the coffin is a clown."[10]

The Owls were officially launched on November 20, 1904, and were instantly popular. Talbot knew he was tapping into a fundamental human impulse. "Everybody likes to wear a badge and receive degrees, have his name in the paper and find an excuse for considering himself a prominent man."[11] Less than five years later, Talbot was crowing about his success: "The second Nest was established in 1905. In June, 1906 it had seven Nests. In June, 1907, it had 68 Nests. In June, 1908, it had 168 Nests; and on December 31, 1908, the membership of the Order was approaching 70,000."[12] A monthly magazine simply entitled the *Owl*, was distributed to publicize the activities of local nests, provide a rough account of Owl finances, sell Owl merchandise, and push John's personal agenda in a series of anonymously authored articles in the front pages.

The first home of the Owls was the Hibernian hall, and many early Owl officers were Talbot's fellow Irish Catholics, but the Owls would be open to

Emblematic Team Suit

No. I-32

This is a great card for initiation work. Has the exact appearance of "The Wise Old Bird" and is very impressive. Much hilarity and clean, innocent fun can be added to the ceremony of initiation of new members by proper costuming. This original design, truly emblematic of the Order of Owls, is made in all sizes and should be worn by every officer present during the ceremonies. Its effect is instantaneous and the favorable impression made is of inestimable value. Delivered to your lodge at production cost and more than justifies the money spent.

WRITE FOR PRICES.   GIVE SIZES DESIRED.

Full-body Owl suit for purchase. *Source:* Catalogue of Lodge Equipment, Aids to Initiation, Advertising Novelties, Jewelry, Emblems, Prizes, Etc., Etc. (*South Bend, IN: Home Nest Order of Owls, ca. 1910*).

HON. ROBERT R. ROBERTS
President, Youngtown, Ohio, Nest, No. 1636, of Machine Gun Company, 10th Ohio Volunteers.

Owl, no. 173, October 25, 1917.

There's so much bad in the best of us,
And so much good in the worst of us,
It hardly behooves any of us,
To speak ill of the rest of us.
Motto Order of Owls

Home Nest, Order of Owls

SUBORDINATE NESTS
THROUGHOUT THE WORLD

FOUNDED NOV. 20, 1904

Elaborate Owl letterhead. Letter from Ferdinand D'Esopo to
John Talbot, October 13, 1937. *Letter privately held.*

those of all religions: "We teach the tenets of no faith; we interfere with no
church; we advocate no creed."[13] Although John would claim to be taking a
stand against religious intolerance, in fact he wanted to be able to tap into the
powerful Protestant establishment.

John Talbot knew how to generate excitement. Newspapers ran ads touting
the many benefits of being an Owl. The striking trio of Owls insignia was put
to use on cards and pamphlets were handed out to drum up interest. The first
group of men in an area to form a new nest were promised lower sign-up fees
and exemption from the initiation rite (which was often painful and/or humiliating). Although they were undisputedly popular, claims about the Owls' rate
of growth and breadth of coverage were often exaggerated. A 1909 article in the
Oxnard (CA) Courier stated that the organization had nests in "Alaska, three
Provinces of Canada, the Philippines, Sandwich Islands, as well as in South
Africa, Australia, New Zealand, India, China, Mexico and Brazil."[14] There is
no proof the Owls ever established themselves beyond the U.S. and Canada,
although there was one nest in Honolulu before Hawaii became a state.

The Owls reveled in pageantry, mysterious activities, and humiliating pun-
ishments, but in this regard they were completely within the norm. As a product
of the Victorian age, fraternal organizations invented the template for those
hungry for opportunities to escape the strict conventions of daily life. In these
secret, sheltered social moments, individuals could explore a darker, wilder
side.

Among the most basic initiation rites for the clubs were a variety of mortify-
ing and seemingly dangerous procedures. They included spanking and a ruse

HOO! -:- *HOO!*
The Order of Owls
Is Here

THE ORDER OF OWLS is eight years old and has nearly 2000 Nests, with a membership of over 750,000 in the United States, Canada, Alaska, Mexico, Cuba, Porto Rico, Philippines, Sandwich Islands, New Zealand, Australia, South Africa.

The Order of Owls is made up of the

Jolliest and Best Fellows on Earth

Each striving to help his brother member to receive his full allotment of sunshine. It has become a great society of men who love to laugh and enjoy life as it flies; who help the sick and needy, bury the dead, brighten dark moments and light up gloomy places. They do good, speak kindly, shake hands warmly and respect the honor of their women.

Reasons Why YOU Should Join the
ORDER OF OWLS

1st. OWLS CARE FOR SICK BROTHERS.
2nd. OWLS BURY DEAD BROTHERS.
3rd. OWLS SUPPORT THEIR ORPHANS.
4th. OWLS SUPPORT THEIR WIDOWS.
5th. OWLS OBTAIN EMPLOYMENT FOR IDLE BROTHERS.
6th. OWLS WILL HELP YOU IN YOUR BUSINESS. THEY PATRONIZE EACH OTHER.
7th. OWLS FURNISH SOCIAL ADVANTAGES.
8th. DUES 75 CENTS PER MONTH; NO EXTRA ASSESSMENTS.
9th. AFTER CLOSING THE CHARTER INITIATION FEE IN THIS CITY WILL BE $25.00.
10th. YOU DO NOT HAVE TO TAKE THE INITATION IF YOU JOIN NOW, AND THE TOTAL COST IS ONLY $5.00.

Newspaper advertisement soliciting new members.
Source: Oxnard (CA) Courier, *March 18, 1914.*

MOLTEN LEAD TEST

No. I-12

It was an ancient custom to punish prisoners by suggesting dropping them into boiling oil, but to ask a candidate to test his bravery by dipping his hands into a pot of molten lead gets their nerves unstrung. He object, begs and absolutely refuses, because he does not know it is harmless. The contents of the pot is only water with a little dry mercurium sprinkled on top.

Catalogue ad for the apparatus necessary to enact the molten lead ritual. *Source:* Catalogue of Lodge Equipment, Aids to Initiation, Advertising Novelties, Jewelry, Emblems, Prizes, Etc., Etc. *(South Bend, IN: Home Nest Order of Owls, ca. 1910).*

that required the initiate to show his character by placing his hand in what appeared to be molten lead. At least one Owl was unwilling to go through with the hazing: "When ready for the ceremonies, it was found that he had ran away, not stopping to put on his coat."[15]

Yet on occasion the danger was very real. A portion of the initiation included a scripted argument among members meant to test how the unwitting applicant would react to a challenging social situation. John's skill at orchestrating drama to serve his purposes was apparent in the exercise. At a Tennessee nest, however, the process went awry, a South Bend paper reporting that "recently a man was injured while being initiated in the Chattanooga lodge, a gun being used to make the secret work more impressive."[16]

SPANKER

No. I-13

Spanker of wood, good finish. Explodes a blank cartridge without injury to the candidate or attendant. Thoroughly effective and safe.

Adds a touch of burlesque comedy to the initiation that harms no one and puts "pep" into the meeting. It is a modern development of the ancient "slap stick" that has been a dependable prop in the theatrical business for more than a century. Always "sure fire" for hearty laughs and as safe as bursting a toy balloon. Furnished complete including 50 blank cartridges. NOTE THE PRICE LIST.

Depiction of the "spanker" in action. *Source:* Catalogue of Lodge Equipment, Aids to Initiation, Advertising Novelties, Jewelry, Emblems, Prizes, Etc., Etc. (*South Bend, IN: Home Nest Order of Owls, ca. 1910*).

Another prop used in initiations was the cause of several accidents. The "spanker," prominently featured in the Owl catalog, was also featured in an Ohio newspaper article from about 1909:

> John Maxwell, the well-known proprietor of the Pabst Depot, was the victim of a peculiar accident Monday evening, which will cause him to be laid up for a week, at least. . . . [He] was a member of the degree team . . . who went to Delphos [to initiate a nest there. Maxwell] . . . was to start a "rough house" in the progress of which a new mechanical "spanker" was used, which was arranged to explode a blank cartridge at the proper time. In the explosion the wad from the cartridge struck Maxwell in the left leg between the knee and the hip, inflicting a flesh wound an inch deep and an inch and a half in diameter.[17]

The spanker apparently failed again when a man in Muskogee, Oklahoma, "was shot in the right hip with a blank cartridge" during an Owl initiation.[18]

Instances of fraternal rituals going horribly wrong were certainly not limited to the Owls. In 1913 two initiates to the Loyal Order of Moose were accidentally electrocuted and died in a ritual, and in 1916 "during the Knights of Tabor's sacred ritual in Texas, an unlucky candidate . . . tripped on a carpeted step and impaled himself on the imperial ceremonial sword."[19]

Less mysterious and certainly less risky were the picnics, banquets, balls, and other lavish social occasions that were a focus of Owl activities from Bakersfield, California, to Rockland, Maine, and contributed significantly to the group's early success. The men's Owls organized sporting events such as wrestling matches, while the women's nests had card parties. Still, not every event was in the category of wholesome entertainment. In Lawrenceburg, Indiana, for instance, a program of Middle Eastern dancing and music reportedly drove a female attendee to dance on the tabletops and attempt to take off her clothing.[20]

Years passed, and the Order of Owls steadily gained in prestige. John Talbot, obsessed with growing the organization (and his profits), desperately searched for men capable of signing up new members in locations as far-flung as Massachusetts and Washington State, Texas, and Florida. These organizers were not always aboveboard. In 1915 in Bath, Maine, an Owl recruiter was jailed for stealing a watch. In 1915 in Marysville, Ohio, an Owl organizer racked up bills at local hotels and restaurants, claiming that the home nest would pay them. When the bills went unpaid, locals protested but got no satisfaction. A year later another Owl (named Lake) attempted the same thing after showing $300 and promising to pay the outstanding charges from the earlier visit. When he, too, left in the night, John claimed the man had no affiliation to his club:

> Letters addressed to Talbot at South Bend brought forth the statement that Lake was not working with the Owls, and an offer of a liberal cash reward for the arrest of Lake. A local business man, who'd been stung, wrote back and reminded Talbot that Lake was undoubtedly working for the Owls, as otherwise he would not have risked $300 in a local bank, even for a short time, nor would he have come to a county in which there was a lodge, nor would he have known that all the Richwood bills had not been paid, nor would he have had letters from the Supreme Lodge in regard to them. Talbot did not make any reply to this letter, evidently considering that he had gone too far in his first letter.[21]

Talbot aggressively protected Owl interests, bringing suit against "pretenders" that adopted similar names. He took the Brotherhood of Owls in Walla Walla, Washington, the Independent Order of Owls in Keokuk, Iowa, and the American Order of Owls in Moline, Illinois (among others), to court and won injunctions to keep them from using the name *Owl* in any way. He ran local ads

This gold-headed cane was presented to Supreme Owl John Talbot by the Brockton, Massachusetts, nest of the Order of Owls on October 13, 1913. *Photo by the author.*

discrediting organizations he saw as competitors and others who tried to imitate his invention. He took particular exception to a burlesque group formed to make fun of fraternal organizations that had taken the name the Keep Growing Wiser Order of Hoot Owls. The performers argued, unsuccessfully, that "the owl is nobody's bird to claim as his own."[22]

Within only a few years of creating the Order of Owls, Talbot claimed his membership included governors, U.S. senators, congressmen, mayors, lawyers, clergymen, physicians and men prominent in all walks of life. Back in South Bend, the Owls had more than one hundred members, some of whom Talbot proudly named in promotional literature. The esteem with which members held their Supreme Owl is evidenced by expensive gifts sent to the home nest, such as a gold-headed cane given to Talbot by a Massachusetts nest in 1913.[23]

FIVE

LEGAL TROUBLE

The Talbot Brothers on the Defensive

THE ORDER OF OWLS WAS GROWING RAPIDLY, becoming popular with those either barred from more traditional organizations or those just interested in a lighter-hearted social experience. But John didn't have long to savor the accomplishment. On February 1, 1905, a case was filed to disbar the young attorney. He had been in trouble before, but this time his license to practice law was at stake.

The suit claimed he had suborned perjury, meaning he had persuaded a witness to lie in a legal proceeding. The codefendants were Lemuel Darrow, a fellow lawyer and mayor of LaPorte, Indiana, and Herman Worden, LaPorte's city attorney, which made the suit a regional news item. It was considered "the most important disbarment proceeding ever filed in a Northern Indiana court" involving "a galaxy of legal talent seldom assembled."[1] The case in question, held in neighboring LaPorte County, involved the theft of a fur coat. Stella Lulla, a local resident, had been charged with shoplifting the expensive item. As the lawyer for the defense, Talbot had produced a woman named Rose Duck, a supposed employee at the store, to support the story that Stella had bought the coat, not stolen it. Quickly enough it was proved that Duck did not work for the store and that Talbot had paid her twenty-five dollars to testify.[2] Duck sat in a cell facing perjury charges, and John knew that charges against him weren't far behind. In order to present a consistent story, the lawyers came up with a plan to communicate with the witness, who was now unavailable to them. When a woman named Daisy Walker appeared in town selling expensive cosmetics, she was jailed on a peddling violation, "although she had plenty of money and a great many LaPorte friends."[3] She was held in the same cell as Rose Duck, allowing her to pass messages through her own lawyer from Talbot to Duck.

Talbot didn't appear concerned by the charges and in September ignored the controversy and boldly invited Darrow to be a featured speaker for the first annual Order of Owls banquet.[4] However, the facts of the case were straightforward, and in January 1906, Talbot was found guilty of professional misconduct.[5] Never one to go quietly, John fought tooth and nail to remain in the courtroom. His disbarment case dragged out for five years, through multiple changes of venue, motions, and objections, until finally, in 1910, John Talbot was forbidden to practice law.[6]

John's brother, Joseph, also faced disbarment. He had been unsuccessful in his campaign for state prosecuting attorney in 1904 but had been elected to the office in 1906. His term began in January 1907. By September of the following year, he was accused of the "willful violation of his duties"[7] and twelve counts of misconduct, involving

- filing a spurious change of venue request to delay the court;
- aiding the escaped Lake Shore Gang members;
- employing his brother as a deputy prosecutor despite knowing he had been disbarred;
- employing George Kurtz as a deputy prosecutor despite knowing he had been disbarred;
- taking twenty-five dollars per month from Minnie Williams, alias Kittie Moore, in exchange for not prosecuting her for running a brothel;
- fabricating evidence showing that the opposition's lawyer had suborned perjury;
- falsely accusing two men of conspiracy;
- refusing to prosecute an adultery case despite having proof;
- refusing to prosecute Madge Cole for running a brothel, illegally selling liquor, and operating a slot machine;[8] and
- refusing to prosecute the operator of a gambling house.

In October, two more charges were added. The first involved deceiving the court in order to obtain the release of three previously convicted criminals facing charges of burglary, larceny, and receiving stolen goods. (The men were later brought back to court, convicted, and sentenced to years in prison.)[9] The second allegedly showed how the Talbot brothers worked behind the scenes to assure a favorable outcome at any cost in their trials. They were accused of jury tampering by conspiring to supply the jury commissioners with a list of people they wanted chosen to serve.[10]

The Talbot brothers publicly claimed they wanted the matter settled but dragged it out by bringing challenge after challenge, including filing for multiple changes of venue. Eventually, Joseph's trial reached its climax just as his term as prosecutor was up and the election season was underway. As his first term as prosecutor ended in scandal, Joseph brazenly campaigned to be reelected. The two issues would be solved nearly simultaneously: his disbarment trial was set to begin the week of the 1908 election.

Fourteen counts of misconduct weren't Joseph's only problem. Joseph suffered from syphilis, and the disease was beginning to affect his mental state. Paranoid and angry, Joseph saw the trial as evidence of a conspiracy. He took out full-page ads in the local newspaper pleading his case. One ad reads, "HE HAS MADE GOOD. In making good he has made powerful Enemies. . . . They have combined to defeat him."[11] A second ad includes a long personal statement in which Joseph numbers his enemies in the thousands. He attacks a local attorney for taking "morally and legally wrong" divorce cases (interesting, since divorce cases made up a good portion of Talbot & Talbot's business) and awkwardly addresses specific charges leveled against him, including a bribery attempt from a prostitute.[12] The voters were not convinced. On election day, Joseph Talbot lost the race for prosecuting attorney by the largest margin of all the races on the local ballot.

Joseph's disbarment case was ultimately heard in Elkhart, a city fifteen miles to the east in a neighboring county. The sensational allegations were heavily covered in local newspapers, and to most observers a guilty verdict seemed to be certain. Those who knew the Talbots well, however, suspected the outcome would be in Joseph's favor.[13] And indeed, despite introducing substantial amounts of evidence, the prosecution was outmaneuvered in the end. After making sure the trial was held in the court of a friendly judge and amid accusations that the jury was tampered with, the Talbots got an acquittal. The *South Bend Tribune* alluded to the clear evidence of underhanded dealing but was reluctant to make a direct statement, likely out of fear of retribution by the Talbots: "The decisions of the court gave rise to a variety of opinions which might not look well if set down in cold print and which, therefore, were better not so treated. That these opinions exist seems to be sufficient."[14]

Surely the brothers celebrated this victory, unaware that more threats were looming. John Talbot's mistress was plotting to kill him.

SIX

—⁓—

LEONA MASON TRIES TO PUT HIM DOWN

IN 1902, JOHN TALBOT MET LEONA MASON, a beautiful but unhappy woman who wanted a divorce. Mason and her husband were "mis-mated," she claimed, and she didn't have much to pay for Talbot's services. However, John took a great interest in Leona Mason and secured the divorce. He then proceeded to cultivate her friendship, buying her gifts and taking her out to dinner and the theater. Mason later recalled how she was enticed into a relationship:

> This slick devil sympathized with me; helped me out of my difficulty, got
> my confidence, threw his charm about me (like a spider or a snake gets
> its victims), lied to me about himself, about his wife, and about his family
> relations; deceived me into believing that he was about to obtain a divorce,
> said he lived very unhappy and longed for a companion who was agreeable;
> made arduous love to me; spent his money freely to show me a good time
> and took me to the theatre and to many others places of amusement. I had
> never until then had such attentions shown me. . . . I was dazed by their
> charms and I was blinded by their glitter.[1]

Initially, Mason was entranced by the attention, the affection, and the glamour of sharing Talbot's extravagant lifestyle. They traveled the country, Talbot often presenting Mason as his wife.[2] She was aware that he was married, but he told her that he had separated from his wife and that a divorce was imminent. She believed him.

Soon, however, the situation took a turn for the worse. Mason reported that after a trip to Chicago where she gave in completely to his advances,

Leona shared two photos of herself. The inset shows a portion of the photograph mentioned at trial. *Source: Leona Mason,* The Character and Life of John W. Talbot, Supreme President Order of Owls, Exposed by an Outraged Woman, One of His Victims *(South Bend, IN: printed by author, 1909).*

he blackmailed her and threatened to kill her if she didn't do everything he wanted. Drunk and raving one night, he broke twenty-nine windows out of her house. Although he claimed to know nothing about it when confronted, he was implicated when his horse was found tied outside the next morning.[3] He beat her, leaving her with bruises and broken bones, and strangled her sister with a scarf (for which he faced assault charges). John often choked Mason herself to the point of unconsciousness, and that was not the worst. One night, while his wife was out of town,

> he met me downtown and induced me to go with him to his office. . . . He locked and bolted the door, drew down the shades, turned on the light (he was in a hot temper), and said: "I saw you today with Mr. ———, and I'll fix you that you will never be seen again in the company of another man. . . ." He took his knife and cut and tore from my body every stitch of clothing, save only my shoes and stockings; then he put my clothing into a satchel and carried it out of the room, telling me that if I made an outcry that he would kill me.[4]

John and his son had a strained relationship, and this photo of them playing checkers was staged for the camera. *Source: John Talbot, Who Is John Talbot? (South Bend, IN: Order of Owls, 1909).*

After leaving her locked in the office for several hours, he eventually dressed her in men's clothing and took her to his house several blocks away: "He kept me for three days and three nights, a prisoner, without food and without any clothing but a bathrobe."[5] During this episode Talbot took a picture of Leona lying naked with a gun to her head. He had postcards made of the compromising image, sent it to Mason's friends and family, and posted it about town: "The expression upon my face in that picture should convince anyone of the terror I felt, and now that coward and criminal of the deepest dye is showing that obscene picture to everybody, both men and women, as proof that I am a bad woman."[6] He told her that if she tried to move out of town, he would do the same wherever she went.

Overwrought and desperate for release, Mason considered burning down Talbot's office or poisoning his favorite horse, Gopher. Finding some inner resolve, she fixed on shooting him and pursued him to his office, where she fired several shots. He escaped injury, and she was taken into custody.

Sensational headlines appeared in the papers throughout the trial. The public were hungry for every salacious detail, and because of her apparent honesty and the sympathy her plight induced, the facts were more damaging to him than to her. In an attempt to promote his good character, John had the Owls publish a booklet entitled *Who Is John Talbot?* Along with information about the Order of Owls and the organization's founding members, the pamphlet was a testament to Talbot's upright nature. It included wholesome pictures of John and his son playing checkers and John with his horse, Gopher, although there were no photographs of Mrs. Talbot. The piece was full of testimonials from friends and business associates singing his praises and attacking the "ludicrous" nature of Mason's claims. From this pamphlet we get a physical description of John: "He is about five feet nine inches tall, weighs in ordinary street dress about 155 pounds, is a little bald in front, has good eyes, good teeth, smiles well, wears a dark moustache, has altogether very good features and seems sometimes to talk without speaking." There is as well a portrait of John's behavior ("His habits are athletic and moral") and a vehement defense of his character in the face of constant attacks: "all the calumny and vituperation that malice, envy, or ambition could prompt against any man has been directed against him."[7]

Mason, with surprising resolve, countered with a pamphlet of her own, *The Character and Life of John W. Talbot, Supreme President Order of Owls, Exposed by an Outraged Woman, One of His Victims.* Amazingly frank, she debunked the testimonials, stating that Talbot had written them himself. She directly rebutted every claim he made of virtue and temperance and respectability. She spared no details of their relationship, replete with photos, cartoons, and captions. She called him "the devil incarnate" and "the vilest sinner, the deepest dyed criminal, the most heartless, cruel wretch who ever led a woman astray."

John was anxious to keep the matter out of the courts, calling Leona "too pretty to punish."[8] His brother, however, then serving as the state prosecuting attorney in the county, insisted. John refused to take the stand. Instead, he and his brother made statements outside the courtroom to anyone who would listen.

As the sordid affair publicly unfolded, it became clear that at least part of John's story was true. He and his wife were living separately and had been for some time. Minnie was with her family in Detroit, sparing her some of the humiliation of what was being discovered by the residents of South Bend. Leona claimed to have written to Minnie during the affair, attempting, unsuccessfully, to confirm the details of the divorce. Mason's attorneys got the trial postponed in order to travel to Detroit and depose Minnie but found her uncooperative.

John with his beloved horse, Gopher, in front of his neighbor's grand home. John's house is out of frame to the left. *Source: John Talbot, Who Is John Talbot? (South Bend, IN: Order of Owls, 1909).*

The press reveled in the story, and the courtroom was packed to capacity during the eight-day trial: "All seats in the courtroom were filled and many were forced to stand. The women, who constitute a major portion of the audience, are eager listeners, leaning forward in their seats to catch all that transpires."[9] The story was not just of interest locally; newspapers as far away as California reported the sensational details.[10]

Insults flew back and forth between the two parties. Mason called Talbot insane. His attorney accused her of perjury. Multiple witnesses testified that they had seen or heard John mistreat Leona. In her testimony Mason claimed Talbot kept a photo album that showed more than fifty local women in compromising positions. John scoffed at the idea, but Mason was a determined woman. She stunned the public by producing the book for the court, proving that her story was not unique and that Talbot was depraved (the scandalized judge refused to admit it into evidence). She claimed she hadn't even been the first woman to try to shoot him, that two others had preceded her.[11]

Although Mason never denied she fired shots at John Talbot, the jury had no interest in convicting her of a crime. Even the prosecution favored leniency, suggesting that she could be found guilty and the sentence immediately suspended. The public, too, was on her side, and jokes were made at Talbot's expense ("He was so d——d crooked she couldn't hit him!"). Stating that they were sure that "she only meant to frighten him," the jury acquitted Leona Mason. With her relationship with John finished and her reputation broken, Leona was left penniless and alone. Within a year she had remarried her former husband and retired from public view.[12] The circus of a trial over, John was left free to devote his time and attention to other pressing issues.

SEVEN

—ᴍ—

DEATH AND RESURRECTION

WHILE JOHN WAS IN THE MIDDLE of the Leona Mason trial, at a time when he was in most need of support, his beloved brother's health began to fail. Joseph and John had been colleagues in every endeavor from childhood. They were partners in their law practice and in real estate dealings and clearly provided each other emotional support in their private lives. There is no one John relied on more.

The election season of 1908, coupled with the disbarment trial, inflicted lasting damage on Joseph Talbot. He may have felt robbed of his position, but his failure to win reelection was fortunate for all concerned. One source claimed the Mason trial "cost him his reason."[1] Over the winter he was sent south to rest and recuperate. John must have been hopeful that this would restore his business partner and closest friend.

Early 1910 brought both disappointment and elation. John had finally exhausted his appeals and been disbarred, which was a frustrating setback. However, the Owls were adding new members at an amazing rate, and Joseph's health appeared to be improving. Although he was able to return home, it soon became clear that Joseph's mental deterioration could no longer be ignored or kept private. To John's horror, Joseph was seen in public, disoriented and confused, one newspaper reporting that the "once prominent" Joseph was "in a deplorable mental condition."[2]

Events came to a head only a week later, when Joseph went out with a hammer in one hand and a revolver in the other, looking for his cousin, Joseph Luther, a water works employee: "Swinging the . . . weapon about, Talbot was asking different persons he met, where he might find Joseph Luther."[3] Talbot

Joseph was featured in a biographical compilation of prominent local citizens. John was not included. *Source: Anderson & Cooley, ed.,* South Bend and the Men Who Have Made It *(South Bend, IN: Tribune Printing, 1901).*

was arrested and jailed. John was forced to take custody of his brother and with the help of Owl physician C. B. Crumpacker took Joseph to Detroit and installed him in an asylum. Soon the family found an elegant institution in Kenosha, Wisconsin, just north of Chicago, and moved Joseph there for treatment. Although these events were reported regionally, John must have used his influence to pressure South Bend newspapers to suppress the story, because there was no local coverage.

Joseph's condition was not caused by overwork or stress but the late stages of syphilis. Since it was socially unacceptable to discuss venereal disease, we can't know who was aware of his condition, but earlier symptoms had to have manifested themselves. A reliable test had only recently been developed, and sufferers were treated with mercury, which was as likely to kill them as to cure the disease.[4]

Joseph died at the Pennoyer Sanitarium on November 3, 1910. An article in the *South Bend Tribune* stated only now that he "was receiving treatment for mental derangement" and "had been suffering for a year."[5] The death certificate

Postcard of the Pennoyer Sanitarium in Kenosha, Wisconsin, ca. 1906. *Privately held.*

makes clear that he died from complications from syphilis.[6] John must have been devastated to lose his brother, business partner, and best friend. Until his own death, John kept a large portrait of his brother hung on the wall of his office.

It is easy to forgive the dead. There were many local tributes to Joseph on the occasion of his passing. He was honored by the Hibernians and is listed among other deceased members in their anniversary booklet.[7] John made sure the Owls contributed to a large marker at Joseph's gravesite. A bronze plaque includes the words, "Was skilful [*sic*] at his trade, eminent in his profession, influential in politics, fearless, honest and able in office, happy in his home. . . . He, with 8 others Nov. 20, 1904, founded the Order of Owls, by which this tablet is placed."[8] Joseph is one of the only founding Owls whose memorials mention the organization.

John resolved to carry on, but with neither a law license nor his brother, he lacked the ability to address his legal needs without outside help. He retained an attorney and tirelessly sought opportunities to regain his legal practice. Having seen that Lemuel Darrow, the attorney disbarred along with him, managed to regain his license to practice in 1912, Talbot must have felt his own vindication was not out of reach.

Only a few years after John's disbarment was finalized, the Indiana state legislature passed a law "giving an appellate or supreme court judge the authority

This elaborate plaque honoring Joseph is unique among the monuments in the Cedar Grove Cemetery on the grounds of the University of Notre Dame. *Photo by the author.*

to reinstate an attorney" who had been disbarred, which created a friendlier path to reinstatement. Previously the matter would have been taken up in the local circuit court, where Talbot had too many enemies for his efforts to succeed. It is very possible that the action by the legislature was specifically written with Talbot in mind. By this time Talbot was counting politicians at high levels among his friends and associates, largely through the work of the Owls.

Talbot filed a petition for reinstatement in the appellate court in Indianapolis. Though he may have had high-powered friends, he had an equal number of sworn enemies who fought hard to keep Talbot from practicing law again: "Three members of the St. Joseph County Bar Association were appointed as a committee to resist the application of John W. Talbot, supreme president of the Order of Owls, for readmission to the state bar."[9] The vote had to be by secret ballot, due to the very real fear of reprisals by Talbot. Talbot's lawyer stood up to the group: "John Kitch, attorney for Talbot, resisted the move, defending the disbarred lawyer by declaring that, although he had committed 'several indiscreet acts' during his career, he believed that Talbot had conducted himself sufficiently well during the past five years to permit his re-admission to the state bar."[10] Clearly, Kitch was choosing to ignore that the past five years had included charges against Talbot of slander, libel, and assault with intent to kill.

Eventually, the names of the men opposing Talbot became public. The first group of three were John Yeagley, Louis M. Hammerschmidt, and Arthur L. Hubbard. They were immediately pressured by Talbot and his friends to step down. In June 1914, two days before a hearing, Yeagley resigned, citing pressing business concerns. Talbot demanded (without a court order) that the committee members and the association president, Drummond, meet in his office so Talbot himself could depose them. All refused. Talbot threatened to cite them with contempt (which he had no power to do) and claimed to the court that all four men were biased against him. Hammerschmidt summarized the situation: "His challenge to me is simply an attempt to further harass the members of the committee and Mr. Drummond."[11]

As they persevered, the committee continued to face challenges. Questions were raised about how the work of the committee would be financed. Hubbard resigned and was replaced by I. K. Parks, who also resigned "after a great deal of the work had been completed." Hammerschmidt stated that "he would not proceed alone," which association president Drummond said amounted to a resignation.[12] A new committee was formed, but other action was taking place behind the scenes. With the petition still unheard, early in 1915 the appellate court held that the act giving the appellate court power to reinstate disbarred attorneys was unconstitutional.[13] Talbot was forced to refile his petition in circuit court.

In June 1915, in Goshen, Indiana, John Talbot filed a second petition to be reinstated.[14] John had many enemies among the lawyers in this community as well, who knew him to be volatile and vicious, and "Talbot . . . met unexpected opposition at every turn in his contest. Ten years' time has not softened the feeling of the lawyers who brought about his disbarment."[15] His enemies won the round when the petition was dismissed for lack of jurisdiction.[16]

Talbot immediately entered his third petition in the St. Joseph County Superior Court, with the St. Joseph County Bar Association opposing him. The trial was moved to the circuit court after it was noticed that the judge assigned to the case had signed Talbot's petition for reinstatement.[17] Talbot, true to form, took it upon himself to collect "depositions" against the character of F. J. L. Meyer, one of the opposing attorneys, and publicly disseminate them, and the impropriety of this action caused his own attorneys to withdraw from the case: "As a matter of professional ethics, and in resentment of Talbot's attempt to try his case by pamphlets in advance of the trial . . . there is nothing left for Graham and McInerny to do, but to wash their hands of the case entirely."[18] Talbot acquired new attorneys.

The case continued to make the rounds and gain and lose judges. A year went by, and Talbot found himself back in the courtrooms of LaPorte County, where he had initially been disbarred. The case was assigned to Harry B. Tuthill, a judge in Michigan City, in October 1916, and it seemed as if the situation might finally be resolved.[19] This was not to be. Meyer, Talbot's nemesis, argued that John had too many friends in LaPorte County and asked for yet another change of venue.[20] The court agreed. The petition was reassigned to Elkhart County, but this time Talbot objected to the location. In the end, another year passed before the petition was heard by the circuit court in Fulton County, two counties to the south of Talbot's home base.[21]

After four years of rigid opposition, all Talbot's critics seemed to disappear: "All objections were withdrawn when the case was brought before Judge Stevens."[22] On November 7, 1917, in the circuit court of Fulton County, Indiana, John Talbot was reinstated to the bar.[23] This news received little coverage back in South Bend, pushed off the front page by the weightier topics of the election results from the day before and the ongoing war in Europe. The *Goshen Democrat* noted that Talbot, who had done the bulk of his business with his brother as Talbot & Talbot, intended to go into practice with two other attorneys, Arthur Moon and George Beroth, both Owl officers.[24] Whether or not he could recruit clients remained to be seen.

EIGHT

UNWANTED OWLS

IN TALBOT'S DAY WHITES AND BLACKS did not mingle in society. As was expected, segregation was written into the Owl constitution, which limited membership to "any white male over the age of sixteen."[1] However, as the Order of Owls expanded, there was interest in membership not only from Whites but from African Americans as well. They wanted to form separate Blacks-only chapters. Talbot was not open to the idea. This challenge was facing other organizations, and most were fighting it. The all-White Benevolent Order of Elks was fighting the all-Black Improved Benevolent Protective Order of Elks of the World in court. The Grand United Order of Odd Fellows (a Black chapter) received its charter from an English Odd Fellows organization instead of an American one, because they knew it was their only path to recognition. Although Talbot was a man who in most situations would welcome any opportunity to make more money and expand the organization, he was less than encouraging to efforts to found African American nests.

In 1910, just across the street from John's office, an African American club owner named Verly Smith feathered his own nest of Owls in a building that had only months before functioned as a gambling establishment in which Talbot was a partner. One can only assume that Talbot was aware of this effort. Leaders of the local African American community were listed among the early members. They included G. W. Bland, head waiter at the swanky Oliver Hotel, along with Charles Bell and William Manning, two of his waitstaff. Warner W. Anderson, a mixed-race physician with a practice a few doors down from Talbot's office, also joined the group. They were soon advertising for members

It Pays to Advertise!

Too! Too! Too! Too! Too! Too!

Something New

Afro-American Order of Orioles

formerly the

"Owls"

PAYING for Sickness, Disability and Accidents from $3.00 to $5.00 per week to all Hoots. **LISTEN & READ:**— Besides the above, we furnish you with the attendance of a physician free of charge.

All For a $3.50 Hatching Fee and 50cts. a Month Nest Fee.

For Information Write **F. O. FINNEY,**

230 W. Walnut St.   **ORGANIZER.**   Indianapolis, Ind

This ad calls attention to the Orioles' origin as Owls.
Source: Indianapolis Recorder, *August 31, 1912.*

as far away as Indianapolis and found someone willing to serve as a national organizer, Hiram Sorrell, a Black actor who had been associated with Sam T. Jack's Creole Burlesque (a popular traveling troupe).[2] Sorrell solicited membership throughout Indiana in the newly formed organization before heading to the East Coast.[3]

For a time, Talbot remained uncharacteristically quiet on the matter, but his ambivalence did not last long. In Atlanta in 1911, local Black organizers claimed that the headquarters for the Afro-American Order of Owls operated out of the same office building in South Bend as the White order. Talbot quickly made it known that no such thing was true, even as the South Bend nest continued to operate.[4]

Sorrell, originally from Baltimore, returned to his hometown by the end of 1910 to found an Afro-American Order of Owls nest there.[5] The Baltimore chapter of the African American Owls boldly used the logo of three owls on a branch, adding the initials *A. A.* above to distinguish themselves from their White counterparts. Talbot quickly went to court to shut them down but ran into stiff resistance. Not only did the Afro-American Owls fight back, but they found sympathy in court. The judge was looking for evidence of harm to

Talbot's organization and pointed out that since Blacks were barred from the White order and Whites were barred from the Black order, there could be no confusing the two. He rightly observed that "the most that can be said is that there exists apprehension on the part of some of the members of the White order, that individuals may be deterred from joining by reason of the existence of the colored order."[6] He gave the Afro-American Order of Owls the right to continue using the name. The matter of the logo was a different matter. The judge noted that "the emblem is . . . more likely to deceive than is the name," pointing out that those who can't read wouldn't take note of the letters A. A, and he required the Black Owls to adopt a more distinct logo.[7] Talbot appealed that decision, found himself a more favorable judge, and won.[8] The Afro-American Owls appealed *that* decision and got it reversed. This final judge, in addition to finding in the Black chapter's favor, placed "all the costs, which were considerable, on the White order."[9] Talbot was forced to accept the existence of the Afro-American Order of Owls in Baltimore.[10]

After this precedent was set, other Afro-American Owl nests appeared across the country, from Tampa to St. Paul; from New York to Salt Lake City. The one place lacking African American Owls was South Bend, Indiana. Without a lawsuit or any public argument, by 1912, these Owls had quietly turned into Orioles (still *O.O.O.*) and adapted the logo to show two songbirds on a twig.[11]

John's actions to defend the Order of Owls from African American membership were undoubtedly racist if typical of societal norms of his time. But if the lawsuits are not enough on their own to conclusively show Talbot's personal attitudes towards race, other evidence exists. One consists of a single piece of paper, a short letter written in 1913 by Talbot's secretary, Mary Ohnesorge. The letterhead is for an organization called the Protective Committee of White Fraternities; the address is John's office.[12] The content of the letter is innocuous, but the mere existence of such an organization, certainly formed by Talbot, gives us insight into his feelings on race.

The most damning evidence of Talbot's views are his interactions with the Ku Klux Klan. Although the Klan had a strong presence in central and southern Indiana, South Bend had a history of abolitionist sentiment during the Civil War and more generally progressive views afterwards.[13] An even bigger impediment for the White Protestant nationalist Klan in the city was the demographics of the local population, which was largely Catholic and foreign born. Despite the Klan's thin base in South Bend, they did maintain an office in town. It was the Klan whom John asked for help in running the Owls later in life, an unusual move for a man who was raised Catholic and who welcomed Catholics into his organization. Not surprisingly (and luckily for Catholic Owls), the Klan declined. Talbot reached out to the Klan a second time near the end of his life, although his purposes are unknown. A quickly typed response to Ferdinand D'Esopo, Owl president, states, "I heard from the Klux as you will note. They did not bite. Nothing I wrote them can be used."[14]

Talbot's repudiation of Afro-American Owls, his creation of a Protective Committee of White Fraternities, and his interest in allying the Owls with the Ku Klux Klan all speak to his intolerant views on race and the segregation he built into his Order of Owls.

NINE

—ᴧᴧᴧ—

A PROFIT IN SYPHILIS

JOSEPH WASN'T THE ONLY TALBOT brother who battled syphilis. In March 1915 John was struck with partial paralysis brought on by the disease, which he claimed was congenital, although this is doubtful.[1] Only half of babies born with syphilis survive, and there are visible symptoms associated with congenital infection, none of which are reported in the Talbots' medical records. The brothers were reported to have multiple sexual partners and to consort with prostitutes, so their lifestyle certainly exposed them to the possibility of contracting syphilis. To do so would, of course, have damaged the reputation of a married man.

In the Talbots' day, syphilis was both terrifying and common, infecting up to 20 percent of the world's population at any given time.[2] Syphilis was particularly virulent among the deployed forces in Europe during World War I, second only to influenza in putting soldiers out of action.[3] The disease spread easily, and the one treatment, mercury, could lead to death. Despite the risk, many attempted the supposed cure, as the consequences of nontreatment led to the same lethal result.

John's son found him on the floor of their home after suffering what most witnesses described as a stroke: "He became sick one night and went to the bathroom, and fell. I heard him fall. I went out and he was practically unconscious, and I picked him up and dragged him back to his bed."[4] A doctor attended him that night, and the next day he was brought to St. Joseph Hospital, where his sister-in-law was a director. She remembered, "During that time Mr. Talbot was treated . . . for a sort of paralytic stroke. He was not rational during all that time."[5] He was kept there for two months before being sent to specialists at the Presbyterian Hospital in Chicago. After only a few days, he returned to St. Joseph's and stayed there another two weeks before being discharged to his mother's care.[6]

Multiple sources address the cause of this episode. It seems clear that it involved the treatment of his syphilis, which must by then have been at an advanced stage. Talbot himself described it as "paralysis of the bladder which physicians diagnosed as due to hereditary syphilis and for which he received intraspinal treatment and from which he recovered in some two months."[7] A physician later tasked with sorting out John's complicated medical history concluded, "Probably the paralysis . . . was due to syphilitic involvement of the brain, and this condition evidently responded to spinal treatment as Talbott [sic] says he made complete recovery and that later [Wassermann syphilis tests] proved negative. My present test has been likewise negative, and there is no other evidence of disease."[8] What had killed his brother would not kill John W. Talbot. In the few years since Joseph's death, a new option had emerged, an arsenic-based drug called Salvarsan. It is likely that John was given this medication and responded well.[9]

Salvarsan was developed in Germany by Paul Ehrlich, who had worked for years to find a compound that would poison the bacteria that caused syphilis without killing the patient. It was first introduced clinically in 1910 and "quickly became the most widely prescribed drug in the world. It was the world's first blockbuster drug."[10] Ever the entrepreneur, Talbot transformed his focus from fighting the illness to making money from it. Salvarsan could not only cure him; it could make him rich. Only a few months after his recovery, he launched an appeal to Owls nationwide, asking them to buy and send him Salvarsan. "He canvassed the entire membership of 297,642 all over the United States and had them purchase all the Salvarsan they could find for him."[11] He anticipated that creating a shortage of the drug would drive up its price, making a fortune for those who had Salvarsan. He was right. Prior to the war, a dose of Salvarsan cost $3.50. By the time Talbot was holding much of the stock, a dose cost $16, considered an "enormous" increase at the time.[12]

He was helped in his effort by the war's effect on trade. The Allied Powers had launched a blockade of Germany in 1914 in response to the outbreak of World War I. Very few supplies or goods could get in or out past this blockade, although some exceptions were made. Manufactured solely in Germany by the Hoechst company, Salvarsan was allowed out in strictly limited amounts directly to certain governments. As the American supply dwindled, the British

JOHN W. TALBOT HAS CONTROL OF SALVARSAN

ENTIRE SUPPLY OF COUNTRY HELD IN SOUTH BEND

MARKET IS CORNERED

The Salvarsan shortage made headlines nationwide, but this one best summarizes the situation. *Source:* South Bend (IN) Tribune, *November 24, 1915.*

were asked to share their allotment, but they refused. The French attempted to make their own, but it was criticized as inferior, and even so, all the drug that was successfully manufactured was quickly put to use in France.

It isn't clear how Talbot persuaded his membership to help him hoard the drug. It is hard to believe that the simple lure of profit would make men risk their reputations and their marriages by buying a syphilis cure they didn't need for themselves. Perhaps Talbot insinuated that the medicine would help in the war effort, although the U.S. wasn't yet directly involved. Regardless, by late 1915, Salvarsan was nearly impossible to obtain, and the shortage was making national headlines.[13] Witnesses described the "sufferings of many thousands of blood disease victims in the United States because American physicians lack

Salvarsan."[14] Talbot was unmoved. Newspapers speculated that Talbot was positioned to make a fortune, provided the blockade held: "John W. Talbot of South Bend is a worried man. He doesn't know whether he is, or is not, a millionaire."[15] In the end, however, Talbot's financial hopes were dashed. In the spring of 1916, the U.S. State Department convinced the British to allow shipments of Salvarsan through the blockade, breaking Talbot's near monopoly on the drug. He soon turned his attention to other endeavors.

As Talbot developed schemes to make a fortune from a syphilis treatment, campaigned to have his law license reinstated, promoted the Owls, and attacked his enemies, his son was reaching adulthood. The younger John had grown up with his parents estranged, and his only documented interactions with his father were traumatic. Despite these challenges, he seems to have been a diligent student and a successful member of the high school's debating team (something perhaps to be expected of the son of John W. Talbot). After graduation, John H. attended Indiana University in Bloomington, the first in his family to attend college. His mother went with him.[16]

Away from home for the first time, John H. made choices that put him at odds with his father. In 1916, as an underclassman, John H. joined the Deutsche Verein (German Club) and appeared in one of their plays. Only months later his father would be attacking a South Bend candidate for mayor, claiming any resident with German ancestry was a traitor to the U.S.

As his father moved further away from his own Catholic upbringing, John H. went in the other direction. He sought out a Catholic social circle, joining the Marquette Club, whose goal was "to promote greater fellowship among Catholic students." If nothing else, Talbot may have been satisfied that his son served as the club's president.

With no personal discipline and unwilling to work within a system, John W. Talbot was certainly not military material. His son, however, was intrigued and motivated by current events. As World War I unfolded in Europe, John H. and his friends found it hard to sit on the sidelines, even though the U.S. was officially neutral. A small group of students formed Company I of the 1st Indiana Infantry, as well as a band. John H. was made company clerk. They were sent to the Mexican border, where General John J. Pershing was fighting Pancho Villa.

John H. sent a detailed letter home, published in the student newspaper, assuring everyone, "No matter how far south Uncle Sam takes us, he can't keep our hearts away from the old campus."[17] As it turned out, soldiering was not as glorious as they had envisioned, and the young men were hot and uncomfortable: "At present we are sleeping on the ground with only a blanket and poncho between us and mother earth." After only a few months, the students were allowed to return to campus and resume their studies. When the U.S. did finally declare war on Germany, on April 6, 1917, John H. was no longer as eager to fight and did not enlist.

John H. performed well in his classes and found his niche socially. Demonstrating some of his father's knack for getting people to organize, he formed a South Bend Club and served as master of ceremonies at events. By his junior year he had joined a fraternity, Kappa Sigma, and as a senior he was able to join the Economics Club.[18] John H. graduated in May 1919 with a bachelor of arts in economics. He was a strong student, graduating with distinction and winning entry into Phi Beta Kappa, an academic honor society.[19] He was now better educated than his father, more integrated into society, and poised to strike out on his own. Talbot should have been proud.

Surprisingly, after forging a path headed steadily away from his father, John H. made a U-turn. He enrolled in law school at the University of Chicago. A young professional trained specifically in law, economics, writing, and public speaking, he was now the perfect tool to serve his father's needs. If he had hoped for independence, there was still a fight ahead of him.

TEN

—៣—

AN OWL REBELLION, AND THE CHARITABLE INSTITUTIONS THAT WEREN'T

DURING TALBOT'S PRESIDENCY, the Owls were constantly defending themselves from charges of fraud and mismanagement. Nationally, Owls had a sense that large sums of money were being collected, but there was no transparency in how the funds were being used. There were repeated audits and angry accusations, but somehow all were resolved favorably, showing no malfeasance. Still, unrest continued to fester among the far-flung members. In 1912 a nest in Cincinnati sent representatives to investigate, but John responded boldly. The men were directly threatened over the phone (the calls later proved to have come from Talbot's home), and Talbot even contacted their wives to ask that they use their influence to get their husbands to turn around and go home. Some abandoned the effort and had to be replaced, but a few persisted. The men estimated the organization should have at least $400,000 on hand and were surprised to find that the Owls owned no real estate (the Owl headquarters being owned by Talbot himself) and had only a meager bank balance.[1] A judge finally sent the dispute to arbitration, and some money was returned to the Cincinnati organization. Challenges like this showed Talbot and his colleagues that it was important that the home nest of the Owls appear to be putting the orders' money to good use. Nests across the country were successfully contributing in their communities, and other fraternal organizations, such as the Moose and the Elks, were visibly supporting the needy by building impressive institutions, such as Mooseheart, a large orphanage and educational facility in Illinois. Although the *Owl* magazine published a short list of office expenses, the amounts were vague and weren't presented as balance sheets that could be easily understood.[2] Owls needed to be shown where their dues were going.

DEATH AND DISABILITY BENEFIT

The Owls advertised that they paid out both a death and a sick benefit to members, as many fraternal organizations did at the time. The funeral benefit was a lump-sum payment of one hundred dollars for the member and sixty dollars for his widow. The sick benefit was structured very similarly to the Hibernian benefit, paying six dollars (later seven dollars) a week for the first thirteen weeks, then two dollars a week for another thirteen weeks, which was the maximum benefit. Widows got a subsidy as well. These benefits featured prominently in appeals to new members, including newspaper advertising and stand-alone pamphlets. Specifics of some of these payments were published in the *Owl*, but they amounted to only a fraction of the money collected per capita by the home nest.

Beyond this basic safety net, the supreme president of the Owls offered up three major enterprises as proof of members' charity: an orphans' home, an Owl hospital, and an old Owl's home. These, according to Talbot, had been a goal from the beginning:

> It is the plan of the Order to use its revenues whenever they exceed its
> expenses, in building and maintaining three great benevolent institutions.
> The first of these is intended to be a home and school for the orphan
> children of Owls. The second is intended to be a home for aged and infirm
> members of the Order. The third institution planned is to be a general
> hospital conducted upon the most modern scientific lines. This last institu-
> tion is intended to make possible the giving of the best medical and surgical
> attention and care in difficult and capital cases to all members of the Order,
> either at a minimum expense or at no expense at all.[3]

THE OWL ORPHANAGE

The Owls promoted their commitment to aid widows and orphans, going so far as to list the care of orphans as a member benefit. The home nest printed up postcards, to be distributed nationwide, that showed an impressive brick building and read, "In this building it is proposed to give Owl orphans a real home." Anyone reading it would think that the Owls had built and were in charge of this institution. In fact, the orphanage was the recent achievement of a number of South Bend women's organizations, including the Women's Christian Temperance Union and the Children's Aid Society. The Owls had nothing to do with the construction of the building or its operation, even if the statement on the card was factual: Talbot had agreed to sponsor several orphans. He published details

Benefits of joining the Owls, part of a small promotional pamphlet. *Courtesy St. Joseph County Public Library, South Bend, IN.*

Reasons Why You Should Join the

ORDER OF OWLS

PROSPECTIVE BENEFITS

1. Local Nest Order of Owls pay sick and accident benefit of $6.00 per week
2. Local Nest pays $100.00 Death Benefit
3. Local Nest furnishes Free Physician for you and your family. .
4. Order of Owls will help you to get a position when you are out of employment.
5. Order of Owls will help you in your business. They trade with each other.
6. Order of Owls furnish you social advantages.
7. Dues 50c, per month—no assessments.
8. After closing the Charter the initiation fee in this city will be $15.00.
9. You do not have to take the initiation if you join now, and the total cost is only $5.00
10. The Owls have public land in Colorado for tuberculosis hospital and camp for members of this Order.
11. The Owls furnish their orphans a home and educate them at South Bend, Ind.
12. The Owls pension widows of deceased members.

in a 1912 edition of the *Owl*: "On January 23, 1912, Samuel Bulliner, a member of the Nest at Carterville, Illinois and Grace Bulliner, his wife, met tragic death. They left three children named Bonnie, Fay and Victor, without persons to care for them. Brother J. B. Powatt, President of the Nest at Carterville, immediately took the matter in charge and brought the children to South Bend where they were placed by the Supreme Secretary in the Orphans Home to be cared for at the expense of the Home Nest."[4]

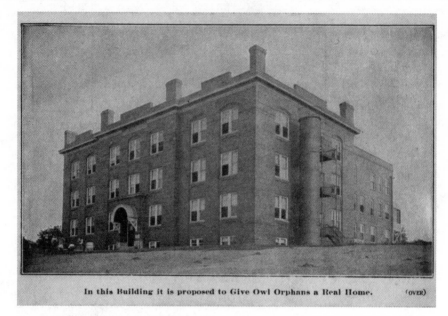

In this Building it is proposed to Give Owl Orphans a Real Home. *(OVER)*

Postcard promoting the Owls' orphans' home, ca. 1907. *Privately held.*

The orphans received small gifts, such as sweaters at Christmas.[5] Although the Owls were committed to subsidizing these orphans, the organization was not in fact operating an orphanage. Ultimately, the Owls' commitment to even these few orphans lapsed. In 1929 the *South Bend Tribune* reported that the Owls were delinquent to the amount of $2,866.[6] The Children's Aid Society would ultimately file liens on Owl property to receive the payments due to them for the support of "Owl orphans."

THE OWL HOSPITAL

In June 1912 a small notice appeared in the *South Bend Tribune* celebrating the Owls' acquisition, for $5,000, of a piece of property to be used for a new hospital. It was noted that the deed had not yet officially been recorded. It never was. The nature of property acquisitions by the Owls was detailed in a contract drafted by the Owl supreme treasurer years later: "Whereas The Order of Owls is an unincorporated, voluntary association, and whereas, as such, it owns and holds in the names of certain individuals and their successors, as trustees, a certain property including the real estate and buildings whereof are called the Owl

Hospital, and whereas this property has been purchased from the general fund of the said Order of Owls. . . ."[7] In other words, the Owls had paid for it, but Talbot owned it.

The property consisted of a large wood-frame single-family home on the northeast corner of Howard and Notre Dame Avenue, a few blocks from John's childhood home. He happily advertised the creation of a hospital as an act of generosity to the community. He secured the services of J. W. Hill, a respected local physician and a member of the Owls, to go east and secure the equipment needed to get started. "The Order of Owls has been seven years promoting the hospital project and announces now that the Owl hospital is 'another dream come true.'"[8]

Talbot needed capital projects to deflect questions about the order's finances, but why a hospital, and in that location? There were already two large local hospitals, one of which, St. Joseph's, run by the Sisters of the Holy Cross, was only a few blocks away.[9] He would have been well aware of it, as his sister-in-law was on its board of directors and he himself had recently been a patient. It seems likely that the Owl "hospital" was intended from the beginning to serve purposes other than treating patients.

A lack of staff points to the fact that the hospital never delivered on its promise. Hill was supposed to run the facility but never did. Talbot hired a private nurse, Pearl Spangler, to run the operation in 1919, seven years after it was acquired. Multiple reports cast doubt on the facility's true function, calling it "a hospital in name only."[10] A Talbot employee said it served "only a few drug cases," while others suggested that the hospital "never saw a patient."[11]

Given the bias on both sides, is it possible to prove conclusively whether the hospital ever functioned as one? South Bend city directories of the period have a section listing hospitals and homes. The Owl hospital never appears in those listings. Over a twenty-year period, from 1905 to 1925, there is no tangible proof that the Owls operated a hospital, with one exception: a single entry in the 1923 South Bend city directory showing physician M. B. Keegan in residence at the Notre Dame Avenue location. This happens to coincide with an affidavit, issued by Keegan, attempting to get Talbot released from prison for medical reasons. The letter features beautiful letterhead showing the building itself and lists Keegan as specializing in "Physico-Clinical Medicine, Dr. Abrams Method."[12] Keegan simultaneously had a practice on LaSalle Avenue that appears in the city directory both before and after 1923, and it seems likely that Talbot had false letterhead printed (as he had done on other occasions) for the sole purpose of legitimizing Keegan's affidavit.[13]

COR. NORTH NOTRE DAME AND HOWARD ST.

This image was part of a letterhead likely developed by Talbot's associates for physician M. B. Keegan to lend the hospital credibility. *National Archives, Kansas City.*

During a later trial, the matter of whether the hospital treated patients was examined in court. Multiple doctors testified about treating patients at the hospital but mentioned only three names. One of these, Mr. Ely, a salesman, was later revealed to have often used the building as a hotel when he was in town. Further, one of the doctors whose testimony was supposed to bolster the reputation of the hospital turned out to be a veterinarian. Talbot also had a long track record of producing favorable witnesses by any means necessary, so there is no way to know if the doctors' testimony was factual. Dr. E. J. Freyermuth, a former South Bend health officer, noted under cross-examination that "at a late meeting of the board of health Dr. Crowe [the board president], gave me positive instructions not to send any more patients to the Owl Hospital."[14] It seems that the "hospital" may have treated a few individuals but no more.

Whether or not there were any patients at the Owl hospital, Talbot certainly made personal use of the building. His secretary, Mary Ohnesorge, moved into the house with her aging mother shortly after Talbot acquired it, and after her mother's death in 1919, Ohnesorge continued to live there until the Owls lost ownership of the building ten years later. What with maintenance of the building, the salary of the nurse (Spangler), and three meals a day provided to both Ohnesorge and Spangler, the cost of running the "hospital" was estimated in 1923 at seventy-five dollars per month, quite an amount for the handful of patients Talbot could show were treated.[15] But of course the building had value to Talbot beyond its purported connection to the Owls. It provided a safe haven for activities Talbot wanted to pursue in private, and he eventually used it as a residence himself. It would feature heavily in one of the most sordid events of his life.

AN OLD OWLS' HOME

A retirement home for aging members was an idea Talbot publicized as widely as he did the hospital, but it was even less of a physical reality. No record can be found of the acquisition of property, the hiring of staff, or any other concrete move to realize this promise.

CHARITY BEGINS AT HOME

With the home nest abdicating their charitable role, the documented charitable activities of the Order of Owls occurred almost exclusively at the local level. Local Owl nests and their members across the United States certainly contributed to public welfare in their communities, but on the national level the order cared for only a handful of orphans in an orphans' home and served even fewer patients in the Owl hospital, and the Owl old folks' home was entirely fictitious.

Even the basic benefits may not always have been paid. In 1919, Harry C. Little, the secretary of the Owl nest in Brazil, Indiana, submitted a funeral benefit claim on behalf of a member. The claim was denied, and Talbot told the chapter that they hadn't submitted enough in dues to merit payment. The Brazil officers were incensed. They publicly questioned the order's finances and moved to withdraw from the Owls. Several other southern Indiana nests had recently withdrawn and reorganized under new names, but Talbot wouldn't let the Brazil nest go without a fight. He published an open letter in the local paper, the *Brazil Daily Times*, accusing Little of perjury and defrauding the orphan's fund. Little in turn filed a lawsuit against Talbot claiming libel and asking for $25,000 in damages. Several months later the court decided the case in Talbot's favor.[16]

Despite Talbot's lip service to the importance of helping one's fellow man, evidence indicates that he was interested in charitable causes only insofar as they served other goals, like appeasing the Owl membership or supporting his reputation in the community. All his personal and professional relationships operated strictly on a quid pro quo basis. And yet a later acquaintance declared, "His life has largely been devoted to charity."[17]

Talbot was a master of manipulating the press and public perception, but he also operated at a time when bookkeeping controls for these organizations were nonexistent. As early as 1914, the Owls were estimated to bring in at least $60,000 a year in dues (over $1.5 million today), but most of that money was never accounted for.[18] Although the Owls are unlikely to be the only organization who misappropriated member dues, the scale on which they operated is profound. Partially to protect the public from this kind of malfeasance, the landscape for fraternal financing has changed considerably. Today most fraternal organizations would be registered as 501(c)(8) or 501(c)(10) nonprofits, with requirements to report annually to the Internal Revenue Service. These reports would be available to the public for review. Talbot had no such oversight.

Unlike the Owls, the fraternal organizations that have survived and thrived fulfilled their promises with more than a postcard or an ad in the paper. The Fraternal Order of Eagles currently donates $10 million a year to charitable causes and funded a $25 million diabetes research center at the University of Iowa.[19] The Shriners are well known for operating children's hospitals (twenty-two of them in 2018) across the U.S. The Order of Elks contributes tens of millions of dollars annually to a range of causes, including special needs children, scholarships, and veterans' programs. On the national level, the Owls at their height contributed nothing.

CAN'T KEEP OUT OF TROUBLE AND OTHER ODD BEHAVIOR

1912: ASSAULT WITH INTENT TO KILL

Always intensely involved in local politics, Talbot's temper was on full display when he attacked fellow attorney John Fisher in his office over a disagreement concerning the Democratic candidate for circuit judge.[1] He was charged with assault with intent to kill, and Fisher was hospitalized. The court record from this case has not survived, but with no further mention in the press, it appears the charges were ultimately dropped.[2]

1913: "SUCCESS IN CIRCUIT LIES"[3]

Around the same time, tension between Talbot and another local attorney, Joseph Meyer, came to a head. Meyer had figured heavily in Talbot's disbarment proceedings, and the two were sworn enemies. When Meyer walked into a bar where Talbot was sitting, the patrons heard Talbot say, "Do you serve c——suckers here?" Meyer slammed Talbot with a $50,000 suit for slander.[4] In what must have been scandalous proceedings, the jury (all male) needed to examine the finer points of what was meant by the word, who in the bar had heard it, whether it was true or false, and if it amounted to slander.

During the trial, to deflect attention from himself, Talbot continually called Meyer's character into question. In conduct that harkened back to the Leona Mason incident, Talbot circulated material accusing Meyer of depraved conduct and even made sure his wife would see it: "That the distribution of circulars defaming Meyer is one of the methods used by Talbot was the charge of the plaintiff's attorney in his opening address. The attorney declared such circulars were even sent to Mrs. Meyer's washwoman, who he said, the sender knew could not read and would therefore take the communication to Mrs. Meyer to be deciphered."[5]

Both sides accused the other of illegal tactics. The jurors had to be warned to report any attempts at communication by either side. Character witnesses for both the prosecution and the defense directly refuted every statement made, making it almost impossible to ascertain the truth. Talbot demanded the judge give thirteen detailed instructions in his favor to the jury and was denied. The volatile proceedings lasted for a year and a half, and Meyer ultimately won. Talbot was told to pay $1,000 and was denied an appeal.

1916: CLASSIC DIVERSION

In yet another widely reported incident, in 1916, Talbot incurred the first of what would be a total of three federal charges. He published an article in the *Owl* harshly criticizing a rival fraternal organization, the Moose. In an approach he had used time and time again, the Supreme Owl attacked the lodge for doing exactly what he was guilty of, misappropriating member funds. Calling the Moose leadership "grafters and thieves," he questioned the extent of recent investments in Mooseheart, an ambitious orphan's facility. But he overplayed his hand when he explicitly called out U.S. vice president Thomas Marshall, the former governor of Indiana and a prominent Moose member. For the first time (but not the last), Talbot found U.S. marshals at his door. They carried charges of libel and slander, filed in Kane County, Illinois. The vice president himself attempted to stay above the fray, stating when asked, "I shall give the matter no consideration."[6]

Talbot argued that he was not the author of the article but only the publisher.[7] He also claimed that since he was not a resident of Illinois, he could not be charged in that state. The Illinois governor at the time, Edward Dunne (likely in return for some money or favor), refused to ask for Talbot to be requisitioned; without the ability to bring him to trial in Illinois, the charges were ultimately dropped. Despite Talbot's assertions that Mooseheart was an empty promise of aid to the poor, the Mooseheart Child City and School is a thriving enterprise still in operation today.[8]

1917: "TO HELL WITH AMERICA, DID YOU SAY?"

Talbot took particular interest in South Bend's mayoral contest in 1917. The Democratic candidate had dedicated himself to cleaning up the city if elected, and that meant trouble for Talbot and his associates. Although a lifelong Democrat, Talbot and his entire family and social circle backed Dr. Frank Carson, a

Republican. Carson's opponent was Rudolph Ackermann, a natural-born citizen with German ancestry. During World War I, Americans were highly sensitive to German influences in the U.S. Talbot played into this wariness, attacking anyone who would support a candidate of German descent and even going so far as to accuse Ackermann's supporters of being guilty of "treason." During a meal at Kable's restaurant (which was run by a friend of John's), Talbot picked a verbal fight with a popular Polish member of the local draft board, Stanley Chelminiak, an Ackermann supporter. Talbot lied that he had heard Chelminiak say, "To hell with America!" and confronted the man.[9] Chelminiak, however, was charismatic and had the backing of the large local Polish population. Talbot's accusation didn't stick, and soon after Talbot was assaulted on the street.

Still, he continued to put every effort into getting Carson elected by any means necessary: "John W. Talbot, link in the vice chain that has enveloped Dr. Frank Carson, the Republican candidate, is threatening to use his great Democratic influence . . . to browbeat, bully-rag, and blackmail everybody possible into supporting Carson."[10] John's efforts were not in vain. A tense election night showed Ackermann leading as vote tallies were called into the papers from the precincts. When the official results were in, however, the totals had changed to favor Carson. When all the votes were counted (if in fact they were all counted), Carson had defeated Ackermann by fifty-two votes. The rest of the winners on the slate were overwhelmingly Democratic. In its analysis of the election, the *South Bend Tribune* alluded to the involvement of powerful Democrats like Talbot in the campaign: "Dr. Carson's victory . . . is due to a very large extent to the votes, in addition to those of republicans, of those in the democratic party who appreciate that the best elements should rule."[11]

1919: A THREAT TO HIS LIFE

One and a half years after Carson's election, Talbot was beaten on the street not once but twice, in separate incidents. The worst of the two occurred in May 1919, when a man attacked him with a lead pipe, putting him in the hospital.[12] His injuries were serious, and although Talbot knew his assailant, he refused to identify him. The newspapers were at a loss to report a motive for the assault, but Talbot clearly understood the message being sent. Although he made light of the situation—"I'm Irish, you know, and they didn't get very far. . . . Either my head was too hard or the pipe was too soft"[13]—around this time Talbot stopped living in town.

Who could John have been afraid of? He had previously shown no fear of physical attack, government threat, or public disgrace. If an enemy had assaulted him, John's past behavior would lead us to expect a lawsuit or at least a loud and violent rebuttal. His silence suggests that his assailant was from among his own associates, perhaps underworld connections responding to some internal event.

Clearly undeterred by the punitive and physical consequences of his earlier libelous attacks, Talbot sent a private letter to St. Joseph County treasurer Edward F. Keller in September 1919, accusing him of protecting "blue-sky operators" (speculators who trade in spurious investments) and insinuating that the letter would be reprinted in the *Owl*. He may have been trying to use the missive as leverage for some business opportunity of his own, but his plan backfired: "Two pokes on the jaw and another in the neck, felling his victim to the ground, and then chasing him down... is the answer given yesterday by County Treas. Edward F. Keller to a letter received that morning from John W. Talbot.... Talbot is wearing a somewhat bruised face and a stiff neck as a result of the encounter."[14]

Most men would rethink their choices after over a decade of publicly defending their behavior, but not Talbot. In the face of the threat of jail time, financial penalties, and physical violence, John W. Talbot refused to back away from his brash, provocative persona. However, he began to consider devoting some of his energy to a new pursuit. John Talbot took on a hobby.

TWELVE

—ᗢ—

NOT JUST OWLS

Talbot Cultivates an Interest in Exotic Birds
(the Kind with Feathers)

IN 1909, WHILE TALBOT was in the middle of the Leona Mason trial, he handled the divorce of a young woman, Helen (Hain) Bartlett of Cassopolis, Michigan, a small town across the state line about ten miles from South Bend. She was the youngest daughter of William Henry Harrison Hain, a successful local farmer. Her husband worked as a carpenter, and her father-in-law ran a summer resort. The couple had been married for five years but had no children. Helen wanted out and, claiming extreme cruelty, filed paperwork on July 20, 1909.[1] The divorce was finalized only two months later, on September 27.[2] As his affair with Leona Mason was coming to an abrupt end (given her attempt on his life), Talbot cultivated Helen Bartlett to take Mason's place.

Helen was thirteen years his junior, not glamorous or worldly like Mason, and not particularly beautiful. She was, however, an intelligent, determined, and ambitious young woman with an interesting hobby: raising exotic birds. She was in fact a bird-raising champion, attending and winning prizes at local poultry shows.[3] John enjoyed and encouraged her attempts to make money breeding Chinese pheasants and peacocks and in time joined her in her endeavors.[4] Talbot and Bartlett began an affair that would last for twenty years.

The affair had Helen's family extremely agitated, her brother Ralph in particular. Helen had originally lived on a farm near her family in Cassopolis, and it was on this Cass County land that she began raising exotic birds, beginning with two curassows she treated as pets.[5] Unwilling to end the relationship, Helen endured harassment from her family that ultimately became unbearable and forced her to relocate. Talbot, never one to retire quietly to a corner in these

Helen (Hain) Bartlett as
a young woman, ca. 1900.
Courtesy Chris Hain.

situations, in December 1917 apparently distributed a pamphlet detailing the
suffering of the innocent Helen at the hands of her "insane" family. Entitled *The
Question*, the booklet claims to be the 127th issue of a magazine published out
of Indianapolis.[6] There is no author listed, and no other issues of *The Question*
can be found; the only identifying information is a request for interested parties to send five dollars in care of the advertising company Guenther-Bradford
in Chicago.

The booklet consists of four pages of incendiary text, written in Talbot's
voice, along with photos. It is pure Talbot theater. *The Question* claims that
Helen's brother Ralph Hain was "going to her home in her absence, forcing
himself into her bedroom, searching her effects, opening her mail and reading her letters." Once she returned home, Ralph "read to her in the presence
of her old mother and father letters written to her by her personal friends"—
clearly referring to Talbot—and "announced that he intended to control her,

Cover of *The Question*, 1917.

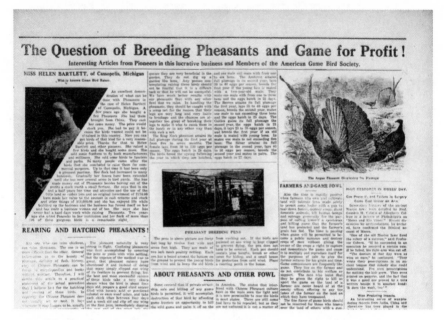

One of the articles John placed promoting game raising.
Source: Perrysburg (OH) Journal, *September 23, 1915.*

dictate her conduct." The pamphlet claimed that several of Helen's birds and other animals had been maliciously poisoned. The most substantial grievance presented was that her brother had "gone about the county talking about her and slandering her and unjustly alleging that she is guilty of immoral offenses and otherwise wrongfully attempting to injure her in the opinion of the community." According to *The Question*, as Helen was in the process of moving off of her old property, her brother rushed in to prevent it. "Finding her in the kitchen he proceeded to attack her. A visitor, who, unknown to Hain, was in the house at the time [Talbot again] rushed to her assistance" at which Ralph "attempted to bite off" the visitor's finger. This account at least may have had some basis in fact, as Talbot's hand seemed to bear the scars of this encounter for the rest of his life.[7]

By the end of the article, Ralph Hain had been characterized as insane, paranoid, a drunk, and a criminal. It called for him to be incarcerated. It disparaged how he treated his tenants and even his dear old mother. Did Talbot seriously believe that the publication of such a piece, intended to humiliate Helen's

This engraving details some of the unique features of the estate of George Jerome, later purchased by John Talbot and Helen Bartlett. *Source:* History of Van Buren and Berrien Counties, Michigan *(Philadelphia: D. W. Ensign, 1880).*

family and containing explicit and sordid details would salvage Helen's reputation, repair her relationship with her family, or stop the abuse? The answer is no. He knew it would further isolate Helen from her family and satisfy his own need to feel he had conquered his enemies. Helen, seeking independence and willing to take some risks to achieve it, went along for the ride.

With Talbot's wife and son living in South Bend and braving the wrath of Helen's family, Helen and John had on November 13, 1915, jointly purchased eighty acres of prime riverfront land just north of the Indiana-Michigan state line for $6,000.[8] It is unclear where they got the money, though Helen may have had some as a settlement from her divorce, and Talbot may have used his own funds or those of the Owls. Fifteen miles away from her former farm and her family, the land was uncultivated and had a rail line running through it, with no obvious use for the couple. Two years later they acquired a stately residence on an adjacent property that they intended to occupy together (although Talbot bought it in his son's name).[9] This expansive property was the former home of popular and influential judge George Jerome, the Michigan commissioner

Purest type Chinese bird. Very hardy. Live in zero weather in open field without shelter. Each hen averages 75 eggs a season. Eggs are hatched and reared by chickens. Mature in six months. Weigh about three pounds at maturity. Free from diseases. Live on one-tenth of amount required by chickens. Farmers friends. Eat insects and weed seeds. Eggs hatch in about twenty-three days. Sell at dollar per pound in market.

John W. Talbot, South Bend, Ind.

Chinese
Ringneck
Pheasant

John created postcards to promote his hobby, ca. 1917.

of state fisheries (a precursor to the Department of Natural Resources) and a prominent Mason. During Jerome's residence, a constant stream of visitors called at his elaborate estate. Known as Jerome Place, or the Sabine Farm,[10] it consisted of thirty acres, with a "villa and tower . . . gardens, vineyards, cascades and fountains," a two-story gazebo, and stocked ponds large enough for boating.[11] It was clearly designed to entertain, and one can speculate Jerome used it for Masonic activities, as he "cut the emblems of the various lodges of the order on one of the small trees along the creek which winds through the property."[12] Talbot was driven daily by a hired man from South Bend to spend the night with Helen, and the property served a dual purpose as a love nest for Talbot and resort for area Owls. After few years, Talbot had a quitclaim deed drawn up that replaced his son's name with his own.[13]

Talbot was a man obsessed with success in every endeavor. His exotic bird hobby would be no different. Talbot wanted to see the exotic bird industry rival traditional poultry raising and personally set out to make it happen. He formed the American Game Bird Society, with Helen as president and himself as secretary, though the organization appears to have had only the two as members.[14] Under the auspices of the society, John placed articles about the care and business of exotic birds in newspapers across the Midwest.[15] If

An image of Helen in pioneer dress as it appeared on her letterhead. *Source: Letter from Helen Bartlett to William Donovan, assistant attorney general, Washington, DC, Leavenworth prison file of John W. Talbot, National Archives, Kansas City.*

the organization was a pretense, his expertise seems to have been genuine. A postcard featuring a pheasant included a detailed description by Talbot, and he wrote an article in *American Bantam Fancier,* a legitimate publication focused on bantam chickens.[16] Talbot even preached the therapeutic wonders of exotic birds: "There could be nothing better for a growing ambitious boy or girl, or an invalid incapable of doing heavy work, than pheasant raising."[17]

Helen's expertise surpassed John's, but he wasn't threatened by his mistress's accomplishments. Instead, he promoted her as an expert ornithologist, game raiser, and lecturer on game propagation. It is possible that Talbot touted Helen's professional credibility in answer to the attacks by her family, but for once Talbot doesn't appear to have been exaggerating. A newspaper article indicates that Helen was invited to speak at the National Protected Game Association's conference in New York, where former president Theodore Roosevelt would also be appearing.[18]

Helen's rustic cabin. Photo included in a 1979 property survey done by the Niles Historical Society, Niles District Library, Niles, MI.

John couldn't spend all his time breeding pheasants. He still had a range of business interests and the Order of Owls to run. While Talbot took care of business in town, Helen happily stayed at Jerome Place, expanding her game-bird stock, which grew to number in the hundreds. Although the main house had burned in 1914, before Talbot bought the property, there were many other buildings that could serve as a residence.[19] Helen, though, had other plans.

Around 1920, Helen had a log cabin moved onto the property from what had been known as the Bertrand settlement, about four miles to the south.[20] She had long indulged a fascination with pioneer life, her personal letterhead including an illustration of a peacock and a photo of her in historic costume. Helen chose to live in this rustic setting, and the cabin continued to be used as a residence for years afterward.[21]

As Theodore Roosevelt ushered in the Progressive Era, the country began to discuss how to approach disappearing wild spaces and dwindling wildlife. States across the country were taking controlled measures to foster the recovery of native species. Talbot found his new exotic bird hobby in the crosshairs of legislators and game wardens, and he quickly developed strong feelings about conservation efforts. To air his grievances and push his agenda, he published a book entitled *Game Laws and Game*, which touched on the history of domesticated poultry and went on to argue against limiting hunting. According to Talbot, the only solution to revive wild game populations was to supplement them with privately raised stock: "Private and state hatcheries make possible the restocking of our fishing grounds. All the protective laws did not increase the number of fish."[22] He also pointed out that the oversight system was bloated and essentially a tax, going so far as to state that "a Game Commissioner is ... merely a parasite."[23] Talbot envisioned game meat on every dinner table and made an egalitarian argument that all levels of society should have access to an inexpensive product. Most important, he said, "The whole system of licensing, tagging, and registration by game raisers is wrong."[24]

In addition to the main text, *Game Laws and Game* contains four pages of ads placed in Helen's name. Talbot even managed to solicit one ad from the Hercules Powder Company of Wilmington, Delaware, which manufactured gunpowder and published manuals on game breeding to support the hunting industry. The book also includes cuts (artwork) for sale depicting a variety of exotic bird breeds to be used in advertising. (John and Helen decorated their own ads, articles, and correspondence with these cuts.) Although the book is listed for sale, since the purported publisher, Talbot's American Game Bird Society, had no listing in the city directory or local phone book, no one who came across a copy would have been able to buy another.

Talbot's interest in exotic birds was sustained and passionate, but in 1918 his hobby brought him afoul of the New York Game Commission, with whom John and Helen had long-standing grievances. In 1915 Helen had written the governor of Michigan asking for help fighting New York's "discriminatory" limitations on breeding Chinese pheasants (he promised his immediate support).[25] When the game commission announced a conservation policy contrary to Talbot's views, Talbot responded quickly and strongly. What exactly had ruffled his feathers? The commission had called for the closure of grouse hunting for two years.[26] For Talbot, this was the last straw. He was beyond making a verbal argument and instead advocated for violence. To vent his frustration, John published a vitriolic article (as he often did) in his *Owl* magazine, calling for the members of the commission to be hanged:

> Hang all traitors.
> Hang George D. Pratt first.
> Then hang or tar and feather in their order
> Alexander MacDonald, August S. Houghton, and Marshal McLean.
> After a thorough horsewhipping tie up Llewellyn
> Legge by one toe and sandpaper him to death.[27]

Talbot was charged with his second federal violation, the misuse of the mail, publishing words "of a character tending to incite murder and assassination." He faced a maximum punishment of a $5,000 fine and five years in federal prison. Uncharacteristically, he pled guilty and paid a paltry $200 fine, though newspaper articles would list the amount as $1,000.[28]

Although Talbot escaped serious punishment in this instance, he wouldn't be so lucky next time.

THIRTEEN

—ᙡ—

"SHE IS CERTAINLY HAVING A FINE TIME"

JOHN BEGAN 1920 AS HE BEGAN most years: embroiled in a personal lawsuit. He had sued rival South Bend attorney Barry Scanlon in federal court for $5,000 in damages, claiming with no sense of irony that a building Scanlon owned near the Owls' headquarters was tarnishing the Owls' name. One of Scanlon's tenants reportedly operated a "house of ill repute."[1] Regardless of the outcome of this case, Talbot's reputation, and by association the reputation of the Owls, was about to come up against a much bigger menace. After successfully weathering decades of attacks on his character, challenges to his leadership, and threats on his life, Talbot was soon to face a set of charges that would finally bring him down, and it would all play out in public: "In federal court today unfolded a tale of immorality, degeneracy and debauchery unheard of in the annals of crime in Indiana."[2]

It began simply enough. Talbot traveled the country promoting the Owls, and one of his early stops was in Topeka, Kansas, where a man named William Bagley was induced to help organize a nest. Eventually, Bagley's interest in the Owls lapsed, and in 1920 John visited him again in an attempt to reengage him. Bagley's eyesight was poor, and his daughter, Pearl, aided him with correspondence and other business matters. Pearl was unmarried, not particularly attractive, and at the age of thirty-seven, considered a spinster. Pearl was impressed with John and flattered by his attentions. She was well aware that Talbot had a wife and son in South Bend, but after his departure the two continued to write to one another.

Throughout September 1920, he sent her presents, including a velvet pillow with the Owl logo. He proposed the idea of a visit to South Bend at his

88

Decorate Your Living Room With Emblematic Pillows

No. 211

Best quality of blue or maroon wool felt, letters and binding white felt, stitched. Owls of natural colors, stitched. Size 24 inches square. These Pillow Tops are beautiful and artistic, and we guarantee them satisfactory or your money back.

The attractiveness of comfortable pillows is enhanced by the handsome Owl Emblem.

An Owl pillow. *Source:* Catalogue of Lodge Equipment, Aids to Initiation, Advertising Novelties, Jewelry, Emblems, Prizes, Etc., Etc. *(South Bend, IN: Home Nest Order of Owls, ca. 1910).*

The photo John sent to Pearl. *National Archives, Chicago.*

expense and the possibility of her working for the Owls. He stressed how useful she could be to the Owls' organization and attempted to allay any possible concerns: "You know from your meeting with me that I am no cad and am not seeking in any round about way to be offensive. Your visit will be to me worth all that it costs and I trust that to you it will be worth all the time that you spend."[3]

Talbot described his young, handsome, successful, single son, clearly giving the impression that he saw potential in introducing them (there is no evidence that the younger Talbot ever met Pearl). Writing in more and more familiar terms, he eventually enclosed a keepsake photograph of himself. Pearl decided to put her trust in John, a decision that would change both of their lives forever.

Pearl left Topeka by train on October 5, taking the New York Central from Chicago to South Bend. She arrived at midday October 6 and caught a taxi to Talbot's office. After briefly seeing him, she was accompanied by John's longtime assistant Mary Ohnesorge to the building referred to as the Owl Hospital

The exterior of the Owl hospital. *National Archives, Chicago.*

and put under the supervision of another Pearl, Pearl Spangler, a woman Talbot had put on the payroll as a private nurse several years before.[4] Spangler and Ohnesorge had bedrooms on the second level; Bagley was given one of the hospital beds on the first floor. According to Bagley's testimony, "she was transferred to the hospital, where she found two other nurses but no patients."[5] She was given a bottle of brown pills and instructed to take one after every meal. The contents of the pills were never identified.

During the first few days of the visit, Talbot's guest was treated to leisurely activities. The ladies went out riding the afternoon of Thursday, the seventh, with Talbot sitting in the front seat with the driver. On the eighth, Pearl and Spangler went to St. Joseph, Michigan, a lakeside destination. On the ninth, they went to a "moving picture show." On Sunday, the tenth, there was another show and a meeting with some sort of "spiritualist" that included Ohnesorge. Five days had passed, and Pearl doesn't seem to have wondered when she was going to be put to work or to have had any discussions about her usefulness to the Owls. She was soon to discover John's true intentions.

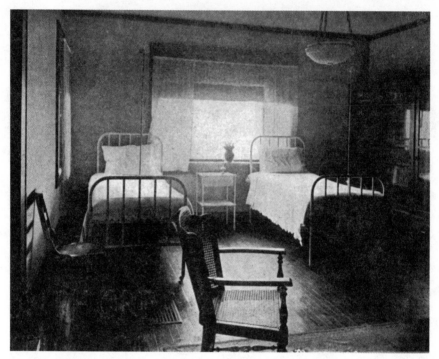

Pearl slept in one of the beds in this room. *National Archives, Chicago.*

On the afternoon of October 11, Spangler took Pearl to Talbot's office. Talbot
sent the office women out and shut the door. The following is Pearl's version
of events:

> I said I must go—that Mrs. Spangler would be waiting for me; Talbot stood
> up from the chair he was sitting in and stepped between me and the door;
> I did not make a motion to pass for an instant and I still insisted that I
> must leave, that Mrs. Spangler would be waiting for me and he ripped out
> an oath and said he had had Mrs. Spangler called out and that I was not to
> go. I started for the door—which I think was the place where the curtains
> were, and he kept insisting that I stay there and finally took hold of my arm;
> I started to get on my coat and he insisted that I need not go just yet, Mrs.
> Spangler had some errands. He had let loose of my arm but he took hold of
> me again and in a few moments he had pulled me down on to his lap. I told
> him he must let me alone, that I didn't want to become pregnant and I was
> sick; he didn't seem to care, but forced me—I had intercourse with him on

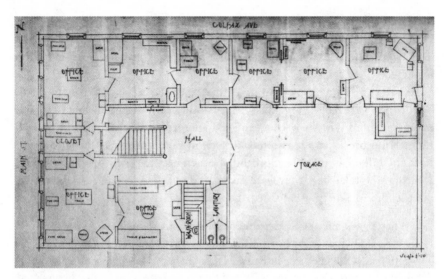

The Owl office floor plan. John occupied the last two rooms
at the upper right. *National Archives, Chicago.*

that occasion in the natural way. That was on a sort of davenport; that was
the first time I had had sexual intercourse with the defendant Talbot.[6]

Later that night Pearl told Spangler about the incident, saying she had been
"molested." Spangler at first made no response and later, when Pearl brought
it up again, only laughed. A floor plan submitted in evidence at the trial that
was to come shows Talbot's office near the east end of the building, adjoining
a small sitting room with the davenport mentioned. A private entrance from
this room leads to an alley outside.[7] These rooms are on the second floor with
windows opening to a busy street. Certainly Pearl would have been heard if she
had screamed, but she did not.

Less than twenty-four hours after this encounter, Pearl was brought back to
John's office, where she quietly wrote postcards before joining Talbot and Spangler at a restaurant nearby for lunch. Possibly at this point Pearl was confused
or still processing the events of the previous day. The next day John cheerfully
wrote a letter to Pearl's father, telling him that "she is in good health, and I believe thoroughly enjoying herself. Yesterday . . . she spent . . . a couple of hours
in the office looking over our stock in the jewelry department."[8]

Talbot instructed Spangler to take Pearl to Chicago, and they left on the
train, arriving in Chicago about five o'clock. They had no reservations for

lodging, and the women had to stop at several hotels before finding a place at the Virginia, north of the Chicago River, where they passed a quiet night. This trip would include none of the shopping or sightseeing Pearl may have expected.

The next morning they went downtown into the area known as the Loop. While they were having breakfast at the Atlantic, two men at an adjacent table expressed interest in the women, and Spangler had a private conversation with them. After breakfast the two men and two women sat in the lobby for some time and talked. Late in the morning, the men brought the women to the Fort Dearborn Hotel, where they were instructed to ask for a particular man, who put the four in a room. Again, Pearl's testimony:

> When I went into the room with this second man, Mrs. Spangler was sitting at the foot of the bed, having removed her blouse; the man was in bath-room. I did not step into the door in the first place, but when I did step in the key was turned in the lock, and I think one of the men put it in his pocket. Then I said to Mrs. Spangler—"We had better not stay here"; I don't remember that she remarked. Shortly after that the other man came out of the bath-room, and Mrs. Spangler told me it was my turn. Mrs. Spangler stayed in the bath-room with the man that was with her; I had intercourse with the man with me, in the big bed-room. . . . I cannot say whether any money changed hands; I got no money.[9]

They returned to South Bend that evening.

On October 14, Talbot told Spangler to bring Pearl back to his office. This time Pearl stated her objection: "I told her that I did not want to go, but she told me that when Talbot called and ordered, I had better go." When they got to the office, Pearl was rightfully nervous: "I did not remove my hat; I was in rather a hurry to leave." This time Spangler remained in the room, and Talbot demanded that both women undress. "I took off every article of clothing except my shoes and stockings; Mrs. Spangler did the same, and the condition of the defendant Talbot's clothing was the same." This encounter took things somewhat further than the previous one: "He forced Mrs. Spangler and myself to have sexual intercourse with him—both naturally and unnaturally. I mean by unnaturally by means of the mouth. That was the first experience I had ever known of that kind. Mrs. Spangler performed the same act, before I did—there was force used. Mrs. Spangler held my head and Talbot told her to hold me closer, and she was to show me how." This act was later referred to in the trial paperwork and in the press as "unnatural intercourse" or a "crime against nature." After it was over, Pearl was returned to the Owl hospital. In a letter dated the next day (October 15), John wrote again to Pearl's father, reporting that, "She is certainly having a fine time, so far as I can see. . . . I think we will keep her here a long time."[10]

On the night of the fifteenth, two men came to the hospital. It was the stated policy of the Owls that if there were no patients, out-of-town lodgers could stay for two dollars per night. On this night, Pearl and Spangler entertained the men, but when Pearl retired to her room, one of these men followed her and forced her to have sex.

On the sixteenth, Talbot again called for Pearl to be brought to the office. At first it was a repeat of the events from two days earlier until quite suddenly John came up behind Pearl and inexplicably cut off her waist-length hair at the shoulder. After returning her to the hospital, he called his barber to go and "cut her hair like a man's." She begged the barber to try to craft her butchered hair into a stylish bob, but the barber claimed he had "orders." Later Talbot would point to her short hair to prove that she was a mental patient, but other testimony shows that he had purchased a men's suit of clothes for her. It is possible that he was planning to relocate her while concealing her identity or that he was satisfying some fetish.

Pearl Bagley had been in South Bend for less than two weeks. In that time she had been sexually abused, pimped out, and had her hair forcibly cut. How much more could she endure? On Monday, the eighteenth, Spangler let her know that Talbot intended to take the two of them to Chicago, posing as a man traveling with his wife and sister, but Pearl had reached her breaking point. The next morning she left the hospital and went straight to the jail, asking the sheriff to lock her in a cell for her protection, believing Talbot would otherwise try to kill her. She had good reason to be concerned, given John's track record of threats and assault. Both Ohnesorge and Spangler tried to talk the prison officials into releasing Bagley back into their care, even attempting to bribe the guards, but to no avail. Two women on Talbot's staff were sent to Topeka to convince Pearl's father to advocate on their behalf. Initially confused, Bagley sent a telegram asking that Pearl be released to Ohnesorge, but after the women had gone he sent another, more prudent instruction: "If there is any reason why my daughter should not be delivered to the officers of the Order of Owls ignore my telegram sent you. . . . do not allow her under any circumstances to fall into improper hands."[11]

While Pearl sat in a jail cell, Talbot questioned her sanity, as he later would in court. He pointed to her short hair as evidence that she was a "mental patient." The sheriff was not convinced and allowed her to stay. Initially (and understandably) nervous and agitated, Pearl gave the prison matron the impression

Pearl Bagley displaying
her short haircut. *National
Archives, Chicago.*

that she was "a dope fiend," but after spending time with Pearl the matron confidently proclaimed that "she was just as sane as I am now."[12] It took eleven days
to work out arrangements for getting Pearl back to Topeka. When an attorney
sent by her father arrived to take her home, he suggested she have her picture
taken to document her masculine hairstyle.

   In February 1921, both Talbot and Spangler were charged with eighteen
counts of violating the Mann Act (also known as the White-Slave Traffic Act
of 1910), which made it a crime to transport women across state lines for the
purpose of prostitution or debauchery or for any other immoral purpose. Since
it took some time for the case to be heard, Talbot continued business as usual,
advertising in the *Chicago Tribune* for a new female stenographer. He promoted

the same rooms that had served as the site of Pearl's suffering as a "pleasant individual office."[13]

Ultimately, the case was tried in federal court in Indianapolis and made national news under headlines such as "Chief of Owls Taken on White Slave Charge" (*Chicago Tribune*) and "John W. Talbot Accused in South Bend of Breaking White Slave Law" (*New York Times*).[14] When the proceedings began in November, the sensational trial was the hottest ticket in town. Over forty South Bend residents made the trip to Indianapolis to see the trial in person.[15]

It is important to note that rape was not the crime John was charged with, although the minutia of his sexual relations with Pearl were gone over in great detail. Transportation for the purpose of lewd acts was at the heart of the charges.

Talbot denied almost none of Pearl's statements and never took the stand. Talbot's defense tried a range of tactics and invented several different scenarios. They argued that

- Pearl was delusional;
- Talbot was impotent and couldn't have performed a sex act;
- they had sex, but the sex was consensual;
- there were too many other people around for the sex to have occurred in private;
- if sex had occurred, prosecutors couldn't prove he brought her specifically with that in mind ("'If he debauched her after she came to South Bend,' said C. C. Shirley for the defense, 'but did not intend to before she came, there can be no case'";[16]
- any activities in Chicago were irrelevant, since he wasn't directly involved in them.

In a tactic that would look familiar today, Talbot's lawyers attempted to "slut shame" Pearl, painting her as a woman of loose morals who was brazenly flirtatious. The defense suggested Pearl had been interested in a man she met on the train to South Bend, that she had a long-standing relationship with a different man in Grand Rapids and made plans to meet with him, and that she had flirted with men on the day trip to St. Joseph, Michigan. Pearl denied all of these narratives and stoically held her ground. In fact, she claimed absolute ignorance of any kind of sexual experience: "Before going to South Bend, I did not exactly know about acts of intercourse."[17]

During the trial, Pearl, appearing in a wig to hide her short hair, bravely explained the entire sequence of events in graphic detail. According to the defense, the mere fact that she could testify to these incidents in court was a point of evidence against her. When asked his opinion of Pearl's mental state, an expert witness for the defense stated, "I would consider a woman able to detail all these things before a jury, without any emotion or embarrassment, to be of unsound mind." After acknowledging that he had never met or questioned Pearl personally, he suggested she was having "delusions of sexual excesses."[18] A second physician for the defense concurred. The lawyer for the prosecution pressed the man, "Suppose that her statement would be corroborated by disinterested witnesses, would that affect your opinion any? . . . Suppose her story was absolutely true, would that make any difference in your opinion?" Shockingly, his answer was, "No, sir."[19]

The public was ready to believe Pearl's version of events, even if the doctors didn't. To them, the main question was, Why did she submit to such treatment for so long? Why didn't she cry out? Run away sooner? She provided an answer to one question, "I didn't holler, or anything. . . . When I get frightened I never do holler, and he frightened me at that time. . . . Afterwards . . . he laughed at me."[20] In her testimony Pearl seemed a bit simpleminded. She appeared to have been completely flustered by a man who acted so accommodating in public and so outrageous in private. Residents and shopkeepers in the neighborhood testified that nothing they saw came across as out of the ordinary. In spite of the unanswered questions, the jury was struck by Pearl's unwavering story and by Talbot's allegedly horrific conduct.

Many witnesses for the defense, all of them Talbot's employees, were less than convincing. Ohnesorge and Spangler were often caught contradicting their earlier sworn testimony. Ohnesorge in particular seemed easily confused, at one point saying, "Some people don't like Mr. Talbot's reputation. I hope I didn't say anything about his bad reputation." "I don't remember" was a common answer on the stand, but when one of the Owls' stenographers, Cora Clark, stated, "I don't remember. I can say that truthfully," one has to ask if she was admitting that the rest of her testimony was a lie. (Indeed, Clark's testimony showed that she had fabricated evidence. At Talbot's request she had generated a letter to imply that Pearl was a morphine addict: "You left your pills here.") One witness claimed that Pearl's hair was short when she arrived in town, despite testimony from multiple witnesses and the barber who'd cut it. Ernest Schrader, a mail carrier who delivered to the Owls' building, testified that a member of the Owl staff "wrote out a statement for me to sign," implying he had been told what to say.

Talbot attempted to call on high-powered friends to come to his aid. Among them was Andrew J. Hickey, a Republican Congressman and former lawyer from LaPorte who had successfully represented Talbot in his petition for reinstatement to the bar. He also relied as usual on brazen legal maneuvering.

The three-story Talbot Building can be seen on the upper left of the intersection, with white painting on the second floor. This image shows its close proximity to others in the streetscape and to city hall, the structure at left with the spire. *Aerial photo from 1922, privately held.*

He filed a motion that asked that the judge exclude all the evidence. He was overruled. He filed a motion that demanded the jury be instructed to find him not guilty. He was overruled. Yet Talbot refused to back down. Despite the widespread news coverage of the trial, in which the Owl hospital's only nurse was facing federal charges, in mid-November 1921 a long article appeared in the *South Bend Tribune* advertising the Owl hospital as a "cozy place to stay."[21] A week later the court was ready to deliver its verdict.

Since the crux of the case was taking Pearl across state lines, on November 23, the judge dismissed the charges against Spangler, given her lack of involvement in arranging Pearl's transportation. Talbot was left waiting to learn his own fate. Strangely, despite having graduated from law school months before, Talbot's son chose that day to make his application to the bar in South Bend.[22] Perhaps Talbot, sensing defeat and potential incarceration, was anxious to make sure his son was positioned to defend his interests.

On November 24, 1921, the judge pronounced the verdict. John W. Talbot was found "guilty as sin" on four counts of violating the Mann Act. He was sentenced to five years in prison—the maximum time for the offense—and given a $5,000 fine.[23]

Headlines like this one appeared in newspapers nationwide.
Source: South Bend (IN) News-Times, *November 24, 1921.*

As was his way, Talbot exhausted every avenue to keep from serving his sentence or paying the fine. He filed a motion in error, basically arguing that the judge had erred in overruling his motions and that he deserved a new trial. This, in the end, brought the case to the Seventh District Court of Appeals, which ultimately declined to overturn the ruling. Despite having assets worth one hundred times the value of the penalty, Talbot was determined not to turn over a dime. To avoid paying, Talbot transferred all of his assets to his wife, his son, and his mistress, Helen Bartlett, before heading to prison, a decision he would later come to regret.

John's greatest concern was what would happen to the Order of Owls in his absence. He could not bear to give up his position as Supreme Owl and attempted to make deals to protect the status quo. Before leaving, he contacted the Ku Klux Klan, inviting them to run the Owl nests in the South, but negotiations fell through.[24] He suspected that if one of his associates was installed as president, that individual would be unwilling to relinquish control once Talbot was released, and John had created the position to be almost impervious to attacks. He needed someone malleable who was simply happy to serve. Talbot saw the perfect candidate in his son. The last detail was settled. The younger John Talbot was left in charge of the Owls' organization.

After decades of successfully defending himself against legal assaults on his character, Talbot was seeing a serious change of fortune. Although this was his first major conviction, people began to connect his name to his many court appearances rather than his status as head of the Owls.[25] Although Talbot hadn't yet realized it, his reputation was irretrievably damaged. He left Indianapolis in good spirits, sure he would not be incarcerated for long. He instructed his friends in Washington to take his case to President Warren G. Harding himself: "Talbot admitted this morning . . . that his attorneys would immediately take steps to secure a pardon for him. The man laughed and joked with a few friends as he left the federal building in company with the U. S. Marshal and his deputy."[26]

As their Supreme Owl began serving his sentence, Owls across the country made no particular effort to keep a low profile. Only months after John arrived at Leavenworth, a large contingent of Owls participated in an enormous fraternal organization parade down Fifth Avenue in New York City: "Stuffed owls of every size and variety were carried on standards and mounted on automobiles. Every marching Owl wore a hatband with the mystic legend 'hoo hoo.'"[27]

FOURTEEN

—⚋—

"GUILTY AS SIN"

Talbot Is Sent to Leavenworth

ON MARCH 3, 1923, two years after he was sentenced, John W. Talbot became prisoner 19003 at Leavenworth Federal Penitentiary in Kansas. An initial medical exam indicated that he was five feet eight and a half, 155 pounds, with slate eyes and brown hair. His intake medical card indicates that John drank and used drugs. He arrived with an Elgin pocket watch, a knife, an Owl pin, a business-card case, and a nail file, along with $113.33 in cash.[1] John had a plan to make his time in prison bearable and get out as soon as possible. First, he would ingratiate himself to the warden. Then he would get trusty status. Third, he would argue that he was too unwell to survive incarceration and appeal for a compassionate release. Finally, he would inundate authorities with positive character testimonials and secure an early parole.

Talbot wasted no time in getting started. He wrote complimentary letters to the warden, painting a picture of himself as a hapless victim of unscrupulous actors and thanking him for his understanding and support. Warden Biddle maintained a polite distance but seems to have warmed to Talbot as time went on. Although he did not grant Talbot's appeal to work directly for the warden's office (perhaps to allow John access to private communications), he assigned Talbot to general office work, a job most inmates regarded as highly desirable. In fact, Talbot spent most of his time in prison in the library and the hospital.

Talbot was granted trusty status almost immediately, which gave him out-side privileges. Since he wasn't technically incarcerated for a violent crime, he was not considered a danger to the community, and no one seemed to be worried about an escape. His freedom of movement shocked his son, who was

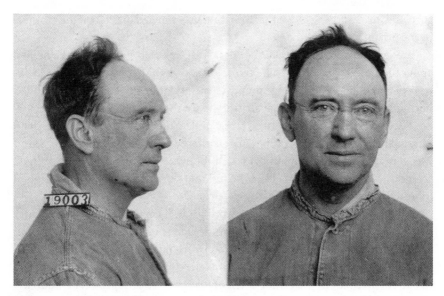

This prison intake photo shows a rumpled and aging Talbot.
National Archives, Kansas City.

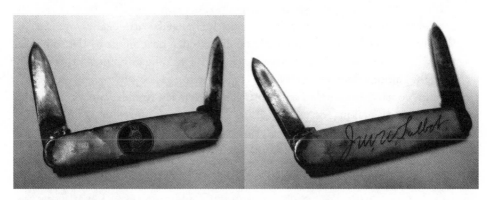

Among Talbot's possessions when he arrived at Leavenworth
was a pocketknife that was later sent to Helen Bartlett. This knife
was found among her possessions. *Courtesy Chris Hain.*

surprised to see during a visit that his father was allowed to walk off the grounds of the prison and down the road.

The groundwork for his claim of ill health was elaborate. At intake he lied about his age, giving a birth date ten years earlier than his own in order to appear older and more infirm. He preposterously claimed to have been wounded during service with the U.S. Cavalry in Mexico in 1878 (when he would actually have been only nine). He produced fabricated medical reports from South Bend physicians claiming he was tubercular, suffered from chronic headaches, and was generally in delicate physical condition. One doctor said he had at most six months to live, writing, "He has begun that slow exit, taking usually several months, natural to the disease."[2]

If they wouldn't take his doctors' word for it, he made sure they had plenty of other evidence for his fragile state. Immediately on his arrival, letters began arriving from across the country, written by friends and associates concerned for the well-being of the prisoner and wondering whether he was at risk of dying in confinement. Even the Department of Justice in Washington sent inquiries, and the prison physician was repeatedly instructed to fully examine Talbot and make a report. The requests began to border on harassment, but Dr. Yohe, the prison physician, refused to be influenced. He insisted that Talbot was fine, a typical report on November 20, 1924, reading, "I do not believe that further confinement will have any specially deleterious effect on his life expectancy." However, in January 1925, something suddenly changed. Without any evidence that Talbot's health had significantly deteriorated, a new report by the same physician came to a very different conclusion. Dr. Yohe announced that he thought Talbot would not survive his confinement.[3]

John constantly complained of headaches, stomach trouble, and a general lack of vitality, making forty-five visits to the physician's office during his two-year stay. Used to the best of everything, Talbot protested that prison food didn't agree with him and made constant requests for his diet to be adjusted. He asked to be allowed to seek the advice of a South Bend doctor, a follower of Albert Abrams, who claimed he could diagnose illness from a blood sample taken while a patient was facing west (Abrams is currently included in the Museum of Quackery). Helen Bartlett appealed directly to the warden for the blood sample, asking that it be sent to M. B. Keegan, a physician who used letterhead listing the Owls' hospital address.[4] These requests were denied and Talbot failed to be released from prison due to any physical condition.

While he was incarcerated, Talbot gave specific instructions to pay his mistress, Helen Bartlett, and his accomplice, Pearl Spangler, several hundred dollars every month out of Owl funds (the only available written proof of what likely had been going on for two decades, the use of Owl money to pay John's bills). The business of the Owls continued uninterrupted, with members Slusser and D'Esopo asking via telegram how they should vote and how to proceed on various issues. John's most telling response was in the third person: "John W. Talbot must be Supreme President."[5]

At Leavenworth Talbot received letters from his mistress and family. A correspondence report shows that Helen, claiming to be John's foster daughter, wrote Talbot every few days. It is no surprise that his wife did not write at all. His son wrote several times and visited, as did John's mother. John also corresponded with his brother-in-law and niece.[6] Friends made sure Talbot was positioned to meet threats against his interests. Helen was somehow given access to negative statements sent to the warden concerning Talbot, which she shared with John ("I am holding in my hand a letter from our enemy") so that they could formulate a strategy in response.

John's conduct in prison was mostly good. His only offense was being caught smoking in a bathroom, for which he was reprimanded. He made friends among the prisoners, including Ralph Chaplin, a radical unionist heavily involved in the International Workers of the World who had been jailed under the Espionage Act. Known as the Prison Poet, Chaplin worked as a writer, artist, and magazine editor. He and Talbot had much in common, both using their publications to influence public opinion and effect political change. Chaplin continued to correspond with Talbot after his release.

While he was in prison, John's aged mother came to see him in an attempt to smooth over some prior disagreement. John seemed afraid to talk to her, stating, "I have for all my life carefully avoided having any unpleasantness with her." John explained to the warden that she had been offended by the speed with which her daughter-in-law had remarried after son Joseph's death, and that John's support for the widow had driven a wedge between them. In fact, Joseph's widow had waited seven years to remarry, and the feud may have had more to do with the episode that had brought her son to prison. In any case, the warden talked Talbot into reconciling with his mother, who died within the year, in January 1924. The warden granted John's appeal to be allowed to attend the funeral. In return, John expressed his eternal gratitude, saying that, despite their disagreements, "she was the best of mothers."

Hannah, with John's help, had accumulated substantial assets in her lifetime. With her only surviving child in prison, Talbot's son, now a practicing attorney, served as the executor of his grandmother's estate. In typical fashion, Talbot disliked the way his son handled the proceedings and disputed the amount his son had deducted from the estate for his services. With their relationship too damaged to deal with the matter privately, John sued his son and won.

With his excuse of ill health going nowhere, Talbot focused his energy on getting out on parole. He encouraged his friends to submit testimonials on his behalf, trying to influence his treatment as well as his upcoming parole hearings. These friends included some heavy hitters: Charles Curtis, the U.S. Senate majority leader and future vice president, weighed in on John's behalf, as did Kansas governor Henry J. Allen. Each letter made him sound more sanctified than the last, but the prison chaplain, Rev. H. H. Clark, reached particular heights as he wrote that Talbot's "life has largely been devoted to charity."[7] However, much to his annoyance, Talbot's adversaries also wrote letters, affirming his punishment and giving dire warnings of what would happen if he were to be let out. Talbot's first parole hearing resulted in his staying put.

Talbot knew he had to keep the pressure on if he wanted an early release. Subsequent to his unsuccessful parole hearing, positive references rolled in regularly, with Warden Biddle promising they would be considered at Talbot's next parole opportunity. Advocates for John badgered politicians in Washington, trying to attract interest in his case from the highest officials, including President Calvin Coolidge himself. Talbot hoped for a presidential pardon. James A. Finch, an attorney active on the national stage who had successfully obtained a pardon in another, equally sordid human trafficking case, went to work on his behalf.[8] Although the president never intervened, regular letters from the Justice Department eventually swayed the panel, and Talbot was let out on parole after serving only two years of his sentence.

Having spent the entire time Talbot was incarcerated seeking in vain for assets in his name in order to satisfy the $5,000 fine, authorities finally discovered that he jointly owned a house with his sister-in-law, Edith. With over $1,200 in additional fees and charges, the bill by 1925 amounted to $6,219.68. By reassigning his assets, John had successfully shielded himself, but Edith, unwilling to lose her home, felt compelled to pay the fine. There is no evidence that he repaid the debt.

FIFTEEN

—ɯ—

THE EX-CONVICT

Talbot Is No Longer Supreme

TALBOT WAS PAROLED ON MAY 10, 1925, and excitedly informed his mistress, Helen, that he was headed home, forwarding his effects to her address in Michigan.[1] He made arrangements to stay with his sister-in-law, since the terms of his parole required him to remain in Indiana, and he was not welcome at the family home on Main Street. Talbot had to report monthly to the prison warden, and these reports show that Talbot did not attempt a return to his law practice. Over the course of a year, he repeatedly lists his occupation as "convalescing."

He returned to South Bend with instructions not to drink and to keep a low profile. Instead, he patronized bars and drunkenly terrorized and intimidated his family. His son, John, in an attempt to stop the abuse, appealed to Warden Biddle, stating that Talbot had violated the terms of his parole. His claims fell on deaf ears. Talbot had carefully laid the groundwork for the warden to be suspicious of the young John's motivations, even indicating that he was plotting to have Talbot physically attacked. The warden wrote, "I am inclined to accept such reports from this source only when sufficiently corroborated by unbiased evidence."[2] In contrast, the parole officer, Timmons, accepted without question letters from several of Talbot's associates, which stated that he was a "total abstainer" or that they had "never known of his drinking intoxicants of any kind," even though Talbot's prison intake paperwork had stated the contrary.[3] Talbot's son got the message and wrote that they would not hear from him again.

Talbot chafed at the terms of his parole, attempting to avoid the monthly reporting requirement and applying to expand the territory he was allowed to travel in, despite claiming relentlessly that he was too ill to work. His request to go to Florida was denied, but potential travel to New York was approved.

Eventually, Illinois and Michigan were added to Indiana as states he was allowed to visit.

Although he stated in September 1926 that he was too ill even to write, Talbot had enough energy to take his relatives to court, trying to recover property from his wife and both assets and control of the Owls from his son. The lawsuit against his wife, Minnie, did not go well. With $300,000 in assets on the line, John claimed that he had signed the property over with the understanding that Minnie would return it once he was released. Minnie flatly denied this. To bolster his case, Talbot produced obviously doctored deeds and claimed that his son was guilty of defacing them. Minnie pointed out that this paperwork was deeply flawed. For example, the typewriter that had produced the documents, dated 1918, had not been manufactured until 1920, and the notary who signed had not been a notary at the time. It was obvious that Talbot had fabricated paperwork (not for the first time), and he lost the case.

The case against his son for recovery of another $100,000 went slightly better, with Talbot being awarded one-third of the assets at stake, worth about $33,000. The fight was bitter, and Talbot was desperate, claiming that he was living on charity. Father and son made terrible accusations against each other, the senior Talbot even saying that his son had at one time plotted to have him killed. The judge stated that they were "like no father and son that I know of."[4] Although Talbot won a portion of the assets, his son had learned many of his father's tactics. He made multiple appeals and took delaying actions so that Talbot didn't receive control of the money until 1930, three years after the verdict.

Talbot's prison stay had been a breaking point for any influence he still had over his wife and son. Now, control of property became a surrogate for personal control. Talbot attempted to evict them from their home, or at least force them to pay him rent, but was unsuccessful. In response, Minnie and the younger John formed a real estate company and bought out Joseph's widow's share of the Owl headquarters and Talbot's former office, intending to evict him and remodel the space. The transaction was completed on March 5, 1926. The loss of his base of operations was devastating to John. Would he attempt an act of revenge?

On May 25, a strange round device was left in a package on the windowsill of the Talbot building early in the morning by two raggedly dressed women, according to witnesses. One of the first to arrive at the office brought the large package inside, recognized the contents as a bomb, and ran for a policeman. Quickly a crowd began to gather, apparently unconcerned about being hurt if the device detonated.

The bombing incident was front-page news.
Source: South Bend (IN) Tribune, *May 25, 1926.*

One of these bystanders, an electrical engineer named Stafford, bravely of-fered to attempt to defuse the bomb. "After his examination he announced that the bomb appeared to be one of two types—either one that would explode when the electric connection was broken, or else one that carried a timing de-vice inside."[5] Stafford must have been confident that it was the latter, because he proceeded to disconnect the battery.

The South Bend Police Department had no experience or training in dealing with such an event. Officer Leo Williams, who responded to the emergency, put the bomb in a basket, and ran two blocks with the "infernal machine" to the nearest bridge. He threw it into the river, expecting the device to explode on impact with the water. Instead, to his horror, it lazily floated downstream. Desperate to render the device harmless, Williams took out his revolver and tried to shoot it, but it was moving away from him. He ran to the next bridge downstream and finally managed to hit his target. Still, the device failed to explode and instead sank beneath the surface.

Police hoped to examine the device as evidence but couldn't recover its re-mains from the river. Authorities had few leads to the identity and intent of the bomber, even though Talbot's son "furnished authorities a few clues that might result in the arrest of the person."[6] Talbot certainly must have been suspected of involvement but nothing could be proved against him. Eventually the police merely "advanced the theory that the bomb was left by someone wishing to strike at the owners of the building."[7] The case was never solved.

John was now in dire financial straits. In desperation he turned against the one woman who had stood by him through it all, Helen Bartlett. While in prison, Helen had faithfully written him letters, visited him, and kept him up-to-date on events. He had even filed a statement that should he die in prison, his personal effects should all be sent to her. However, John's relationship with Helen had turned sour after his release. Starting in November 1925, Talbot

Drops Bomb Into River

Officer Leo Williams dropped the bomb into the St. Joseph river, after it was taken from the Talbot bldg. at Main and Colfax, where it had been planted by some one whose identity the police are attempting to establish. (Photo by Elmore, News-Times staff cameraman.)

Officer Williams was happy to reenact his role in the event for reporters. *Source: South Bend (IN) News-Times, May 25, 1926.*

began showing up at her home, drunk, abusive, and threatening (behavior commonly attributed to him). A written complaint was made to the warden, who notified John's parole officer to look into the matter.[8] The parole officer found it difficult to contact Talbot or his sponsoring in-laws, who claimed they were all quarantining due to smallpox. The officer accepted the written assurance of John's sponsor that, "regarding his association with a Niles woman [remember, Bartlett was supposed to have been Talbot's foster daughter] I can state from good authority that he has not been in Niles in the past two months."[9] A letter sent to Washington concerning Talbot's behavior resulted in an investigation by two U.S. marshals. One, reporting that "his reputation is not good," stopped short of advising Talbot be returned to prison but suggested his permission to travel to Michigan be revoked.[10] His parole officer warned him to "walk so straight that you bend backwards."[11] Although the claims of abuse were never substantiated, it was clear that Helen and John were no longer on good terms.

Talbot filed suit against his mistress in April 1926, asking for the return of the property he had signed over to her before going to prison, but Helen, like Minnie, was determined to put up a fight. Not only did she staunchly defend her interests in court, she also took drastic steps to change her personal situation. Whether because she was trying to protect her assets or because she was frightened, within a few weeks of being taken to court Helen suddenly married Joseph Wartha, a widowed Hungarian Catholic with three children.[12] It may have been helpful that he was a former deputy U.S. marshal (although he had been discharged for bootlegging).[13]

Talbot took steps to protect himself from further reports of misconduct by his former mistress. He wrote the parole officer and the warden, hoping to "lighten their burden" by warning them of a groundswell of resentment towards him due to the litigation and suggesting the opposing parties were lying to help their own cause. It seems to have worked, because there is no further evidence that Officer Timmons resumed investigations into Talbot.

Claiming that $100,000 in assets had been turned over to her with the understanding they would be returned, John took Helen to court in Michigan. She produced documents showing that the property had been legally transferred. She also stated that there had been a mutual agreement, and that Talbot was given $4,000 in bonds in return for the property. John admitted there had been an agreement but denied he had received the bonds. The judge concluded that someone must be lying and clearly thought it was Talbot, calling it, "The most flagrant case of perjury I have ever listened to in this court."[14] The judge suspended the case until the truth of the matter could be determined.

Talbot realized that he had misjudged the situation and that he might be in serious trouble, possibly even facing a return to prison. The man who had up until this moment brazenly faced every challenge did something completely out of character. He disappeared.[15]

Rumors spread that he had gone west, perhaps to Arizona or Utah, perhaps even Mexico. Federal marshals went on the hunt, asking the surprised Leavenworth officials (they had been convinced that John was an honest man) for descriptive information to assist them in their search. Eventually, Talbot was discovered in Vincennes, Indiana. He had been admitted to the Knox County bar under the name John Devine (a name borrowed from a Notre Dame track star and South Bend attorney), but he was hardly keeping his head down: "He

resorted to 'ambulance chasing' and soon was banned by several organizations."[16] The marshals brought Talbot back to Grand Rapids, where, denied
bond, he sat in jail for months, waiting to face perjury charges.

In May 1928 the suit against Helen was dismissed, and she was awarded
court costs.[17] The assets now safely under her control, Helen happily assisted
the court with the perjury charge. Although Bartlett introduced bank records
and the testimony of banking officials to support her version of events, in October the perjury case against Talbot was dismissed.[18] A relieved Talbot retreated
to South Bend.

After unsuccessfully seeking the return of nearly half a million dollars'
worth of assets he had willingly signed away to his wife, his son, and his mistress, Talbot was left with a tiny fraction of his former wealth and lacked access
to the source of his power, control of the Owls. He gathered himself to fight
for his fowl.

Assets weren't the only thing Talbot had to protect when he was sent to
prison. The Order of Owls required attention and an unincarcerated president,
a problem Talbot thought he had solved by promoting his malleable son to the
position of Supreme Owl. Sensing his opportunity, Ferdinand D'Esopo, the
president of the Hartford, Connecticut, nest, attempted to install himself as
president of the organization. The younger Talbot barely maintained control
with the help of Talbot's faithful office manager, Mary Ohnesorge. Talbot may
have initially been pleased, but over time he grew to regret his decision.

John H. Talbot knew he could not remain in control of the Owls once his
father was released. Enjoying his power and mindful of his finances, he tried
to lead those aligned with him into a new organization, the Order of Otters,
which his father of course vehemently opposed.[19] The venture failed, leaving
John H. to face off against his father.

For years, the senior Talbot had masterfully manipulated Owl assets for
his own benefit, fighting off every attempt to force him to account for the huge
amounts of money submitted to the national home nest. The younger Talbot
ran the organization on his father's model but without his father's skills in manipulation and deception. He knew the other officers were loyal to his father
and moved to have them replaced. Talbot filed a lawsuit to put an end to this
behavior. In court Talbot accused his son of paying himself and the other officers thousands of dollars a year, in violation of the Owl constitution (though
Talbot had likely done the same). Talbot questioned how his friends had been
forced out of office and why he was foiled in his attempts to vote by proxy while
in prison.

The court found that the younger Talbot was within his rights but was reluctant to issue a ruling, instead sending the matter to arbitration. The situation became even more volatile when Talbot threw his support to D'Esopo. Eventually, the suit was settled in the U.S. district court in Indianapolis with a surprise ruling in 1929: Neither Talbot would run the organization. D'Esopo would be named supreme president, and the center of the organization would move from South Bend to Hartford.[20] The river of money and influence that had fueled Talbot's life would cease to flow. He had lost control of the organization he had brought into being twenty-five years before.

SIXTEEN

—ꝏ—

A QUIETER LIFE

JOHN W. TALBOT HAD LOST EVERYTHING: his fortune, his influence, and any pretense of a reputation. He told his parole officer he was setting up a new luncheon club, called the Associated Advance Club, but this effort either failed or was a lie to satisfy his parole officer. Attempting to go back into business, he had trouble finding an office building that would allow him as a tenant. Eventually, he set up practice in the Platt Building, an unimpressive, three-story office building on the southern end of downtown South Bend. Once his parole expired and he was allowed to leave, he moved out of his sister-in-law's house and into the former Owl "hospital." Initially, he shared it with Mary Ohnesorge, his faithful secretary, but she soon moved to Michigan and died there only a few years later.[1] Talbot kept the Order of Owls nest number one in operation, listing himself as secretary and using his office as its mailing address. It is unclear how active the nest was, if it was at all. By 1932 many of the founding members of the Owls were dead or had left the organization, and John's shattered reputation would have tainted anyone who associated with him.

At one time reported to be worth half a million dollars, John Talbot had spent lavishly on food, entertainment, travel, and women but apparently failed to pay the lawyers who represented him after his disbarment left him unable to represent himself. At least two of his lawyers took him to court themselves. Jonas Hoover, the Chicago attorney who represented him in the Leona Mason case, sued him for payment. Otis Romine, the local attorney who represented him in asset trials with his family, claimed most of the money that Talbot was awarded and ultimately filed a tax lien to try to take care of the balance, but the Children's Aid Society (the operators of the home where the Owls had sent orphans) beat him to the punch. In 1933 the court awarded the Owl "hospital" to the society to cover unpaid orphan fees. John was forced to move into his office space, which would serve as his final residence.

Throughout his life, John Talbot's behavior failed to conform to societal norms. Can John's actions be explained by hereditary psychological issues? Other members of John's family appear to have struggled with mental illness. Two of John's first cousins committed suicide, and the death of a third was "complicated by depressive psychosis."[2] Another cousin killed his friend and neighbor in a dramatic episode that was quickly swept under the carpet.[3] Is it possible that John suffered from manic depression? Although there is certainly evidence of mania, there is no evidence that Talbot ever sought to end his life, and neither his friends nor his enemies ever describe him as depressed.

Could his behavior have been the result of a disease? Symptoms of the later stages of syphilis include paranoia, mood swings, and personality changes, and Talbot's medical records show that he was treated for the disease. Yet John lived for more than twenty years after his diagnosis. At the time, it was rare but possible to recover from this advanced stage of the disease. If his syphilis was indeed cured in 1915, then the disease does not explain his conduct.

Did Talbot suffer a life-altering injury? Lawyers at Talbot's Mann Act trial seem to have been attempting to introduce evidence that a serious head injury had affected his personality and behavior. Witnesses at that trial and medical reports created during his stay in Leavenworth, along with his own accounts, all concur that he had suffered brain trauma and that his health and temperament had changed as a result. His relatives state that it was a result of the beating with a lead pipe documented in local newspapers. Talbot himself said he had been kicked in the head by a horse. Both of these may have been true, but the Leona Mason trial and other incidents show that Talbot was committing questionable acts long before any head injury occurred.

Was Talbot insane? As early as 1909 and again in 1912, his sanity was legally questioned in court, and newspaper headlines included statements like "Is Talbot Crazy?"[4] It was obvious that he was immoral, erratic, and sometimes violent, and his behavior was far outside the norm, yet he was a successful professional, the leader of a large organization. The answer to the question of whether Talbot was mentally ill is quite possibly yes.

From the time he was a teenager to the time of his death, John W. Talbot consistently broke the law, manipulated the people around him, and displayed no capacity for empathy or remorse. In fact, his actions appear to match those of someone who would today be formally classified as a psychopath:[5]

- A disregard for laws and social mores
- A disregard for the rights of others
- A failure to feel remorse or guilt
- A tendency to display violent behavior

One description of psychopathic behavior sounds as if it could have been written with Talbot in mind: "Psychopaths . . . are unable to form emotional attachments or feel real empathy with others, although they often have disarming or even charming personalities. . . . Psychopaths are very manipulative and can easily gain people's trust. [They] are often educated and hold steady jobs. . . . When committing crimes, psychopaths carefully plan out every detail in advance and often have contingency plans in place. Unlike their sociopathic counterparts, psychopathic criminals are cool, calm, and meticulous. Their crimes, whether violent or non-violent, will be highly organized."[6] It is impossible to diagnose a subject remotely, let alone from beyond the grave, but it seems likely that Talbot simply lacked the ability to act within a moral code or to understand the harm he was inflicting on those around him. Today he might be described as having an antisocial personality disorder or psychopathic tendencies.

By 1934 Talbot was sixty-five years old. Whatever the cause, his actions since boyhood had resulted in a trail of destruction in both his personal and professional worlds. He had spent his life frantically working to bring a multitude of schemes to fruition, but everything he had worked for was gone. He had made and lost a fortune, along with many powerful friends and his family. With little work and no ventures to occupy his time, Talbot spent his final days and nights in his office, usually drinking heavily.

SEVENTEEN

—⚋—

A FIERY DEATH

TALBOT'S HEALTH WAS SERIOUSLY IN DECLINE, the result of a lifetime of alcohol abuse and other excesses. He required the aid of crutches to walk and suffered from abdominal pain. Using Owl letterhead, he wrote to William Lowe Bryan, the president of Indiana University, hoping for a referral to a medical professional, although he indicated he was asking for a "friend." He explained the symptoms: "His difficulty appears to be in the region of the liver and gall. He suffers much pain. . . . He has lost much weight. He is very week [sic] and physical exertion quickly wears him out."[1] He pointed out that his "friend" couldn't afford any great expense. Bryan, likely puzzled that Talbot had sent such a request to the president of a university, nevertheless responded quickly, referring John to the head of the Indiana University School of Medicine but noting that there was a long waiting list. Bryan didn't offer any special assistance.[2]

On December 14, 1937, Talbot ate, as he often did, at his desk, a large rolltop, its pigeonholes stuffed with papers. He had been living in a suite of three small rooms that served as his office for years, unable to afford a better situation and unwelcome at the home of his wife and son. He had whiskey with his meal, as usual, and soon drank himself into a stupor. On this night his smoldering cigarette fell into a trash can below his desk, setting some papers on fire. Talbot was too drunk to notice. "The blaze was discovered at 7:30 p.m. by Ross L. Jordan. . . . Noticing smoke drifting into the corridor, he opened the door and saw the office ablaze and Mr. Talbot seated at the desk, his clothing afire."[3] Investigators were amazed that there was no evidence that John had awoken or made any effort to escape the inferno. He died consumed by flame, his body burned "almost beyond recognition."

Talbot's dramatic death received sensational coverage.
Source: South Bend (IN) Tribune, *December 15, 1937.*

Realizing that Talbot had many enemies and that there was a possibility of foul play, the county coroner photographed the body and the scene from every angle possible but found no wounds or evidence of bodily injury prior to the fire. Witnesses claimed that Talbot's intoxication was a common occurrence and that he had barely escaped lighting a blaze with his cigarettes on multiple previous occasions. As stated in the report, "He was addicted to alcohol and a bottle half full of liquor was found on his desk immediately after death. He was in the habit of falling asleep in his intoxicated states and remained at his desk until he regained consciousness. He was also quite a persistent smoker and used chiefly cigarettes." The coroner's conclusion was accidental death.[4]

For the last time, John W. Talbot was featured on the front page of the local paper, which spent four columns covering the remarkable events of his life and death. They included graphic images of the burned desk, along with a portrait and a photo of him with his favorite horse. His death made national news as well, the *New York Times*, the *Chicago Tribune*, and other papers picking up the story. Many of the articles emphasized Talbot's fall from grace: "Once reputedly a millionaire, he was said to be virtually penniless."[5]

John was survived by his wife and son, but his family had no role in placing a traditional obituary or planning the funeral. Instead, the Owl home nest in

This headstone marks Talbot's grave in South Bend's City Cemetery. *Photo by the author.*

Hartford took on the arrangements. There was a short service at the funeral home, followed by burial in South Bend's City Cemetery. It was unusual for a Catholic to be interred at this Protestant cemetery, but Talbot had long since abandoned the Church.

His gravesite, part of a plot that belonged to the Owls, was intended for indigent members. When he arranged to buy the plot, Talbot could not have conceived that he would end up buried in it, nor would he have guessed the company he would keep in death. Talbot is interred next to two felons, Thomas Conway and Frank Webb. Conway is likely the same man involved in activities of the Irish mob in Chicago, although newspaper reports of his death while visiting South Bend identify him as a journalist. Webb was reported to be a member of the Lake Shore Gang and had died in the Michigan City prison serving time for murdering a sheriff in Pulaski County after robbing a store.[6]

The men Talbot aspired to spend his time with were those he considered his peers, those who wielded power and influence, who were looked up to by society. In fact, he surrounded himself with petty criminals and sycophants, and his neighbors in death are men who were more truly his equals. Conway and Webb have Owl engravings on their gravestones. Talbot's small granite marker makes no mention of the Owls.

After a turbulent life, John may have finally found peace. Throughout his life, he seemed to idealize death. Consider this excerpt from a speech delivered by Talbot at an Owls' memorial service in November 1909:

> The dead! *Our* dead. What those words mean can never be expressed. Health may be lost and fortune disappear, but *God Himself has not the power to rob us of our dead.* No face or form can win from us *our dead.* They are beyond the seducer's charms and the despoiler's hands. *** To age, when toys and dreams and plans are gone, is given reality—the only thing that never changes—the only thing that will endure—*our dead.* *** Without our dead, sentiment would not exist; beauty would be unknown. *We would not care for immortality but that we hope to meet our dead.* They are the inspiration for religion; the source of lasting hope. Life would be death, and death would be eternal, without our dead. In graves their bodies may be turned to dust—to us they never change. In walks, in drives, in storms, in calms, in smiles, in tears, in comforting and love, they live—and live—*and live*—and cannot die or change—*our dead.*[7]

Death seemed to be always on Talbot's mind. The October 1917 issue of the *Owl* included part of a poem by Paul Laurence Dunbar entitled "Mortality":

> Ashes to ashes, dust unto dust,
> What of his loving, what of his lust?
> What of his passion, what of his pain?
> What of his poverty, what of his pride?
> Earth, the great mother, has called him again:
> Deeply he sleeps, the world's verdict defied.
> Shall he be tried again? Shall he go free?
> What [Who] shall the court convene?
> Where shall it be?

EIGHTEEN

—◠◡◠—

THE FATE OF THE ORDER OF OWLS

THE HISTORY OF THE OWLS can be divided into three eras: the rise of the Owls, the decline under Talbot, and the time after Talbot. From its founding in 1904 up through World War I, the Owls expanded briskly, adding nests and members at an astonishing rate. Discussions of fraternal activity nationwide included the Order of Owls among the top organizations. John's charisma and manic work ethic drove this early success and rapid growth. He personally oversaw the extensive network of operatives who solicited new members. He worked tirelessly to promote the organization—writing letters, distributing ad copy, traveling extensively, and selling Owl merchandise.

Two factors contributed to the order's decline while Talbot was still in charge. The first was the obvious problem of the integrity of the leadership. There were questions about the organization's finances almost from the beginning, which drove some local nests to close down or adopt different affiliations. In the early years Talbot was always able to control the narrative enough to keep these disputes localized, and his personal accomplishments were often touted in public recruitments. However, over time his never-ending personal battles and court appearances cast more and more doubt on the nature of his character and his ability to lead the Owls. This came to a head during Talbot's well-publicized "white slavery" trial. When Talbot could no longer employ his own clout and in fact became a detriment in membership appeals, the Owls' growth slowed considerably.

As John's behavior became more erratic and his reputation worsened, he began to struggle to retain and motivate the rest of the Owl leadership. His closest associates had trouble standing by him. Most of the Owl founders eventually attempted to disassociate themselves from the organization and from Talbot. John J. Johnson, supreme invocator, was the first to go, moving to Alabama in 1910. Within a few years, he was dead as a result of injuries he received in an accident. At this early date, the Owls still feature prominently in his obituary. [1]

George Beroth, supreme secretary, had had enough in the mid-1910s but found that leaving the organization put him on Talbot's target list. Unwilling or unable to withstand John's attacks, he gave up law entirely and left South Bend for Hartford, Connecticut, to start a bakery. His obituary mentions his involvement in the Knights of Pythias and the Masons but not the Owls. This became typical of all the remaining founders. The obituary of J. Lott Losey, once the supreme treasurer and the Owl jeweler, includes no reference to the Owls. Similarly, the death notice for Chester B. Crumpacker, formerly the supreme vice president, only lists membership in organizations other than the Owls. Membership in the Owls had ceased to be a point of pride for these men.

The second factor in the Owls' decline under Talbot had nothing to do with him. Interest in fraternal organizations flagged nationwide during the 1920s. Much of their early appeal was that the groups provided members a private venue to let go of inhibitions during an extremely restrictive era, but World War I changed societal norms. After the war, expectations of appropriate behavior were different, more lenient. It was the Jazz Age, and public intoxication, dancing, and relations between women and men became much more permissive. As a result, membership in fraternal organizations offered a less singular opportunity. Not just the Owls but fraternal organizations across the board saw a drop in popularity.

John Talbot served as Supreme Owl for the first twenty-five years of the Order of Owls' existence; he founded the Order, saw the organization achieve national prominence, and then watched membership dwindle. He lost the title in 1929 to Ferdinand D'Esopo, although the two continued to communicate and collaborate on Owl activities.[2] When D'Esopo took control of the Owls, the headquarters was moved to his home base of Hartford, Connecticut. He remained Supreme Owl for several decades. His legal career and record of involvement in local politics and other local fraternal organizations show none of the scandalous behavior or nefarious business practices that were characteristic of Talbot.[3] However, he also lacked John's creativity and magnetism and was unable to make joining the Owls seem as desirable as had his predecessor. Without John's talents and in the face of more established, less troubled competitors, the Owls began to fade. The Owls would never again reach the heights they had under Talbot's dubious leadership. At their zenith, they claimed nine hundred thousand members, though they never reached the mainstream status

Owl building shortly before it was demolished to make way for a parking structure.
Photo courtesy of the History Museum, South Bend, Indiana.

of groups like the Moose and Elks. This outcome was not preordained. If Talbot had been able to continue to devote his energy and enthusiasm to the organization instead of his personal problems, the organization would have retained its high profile. If Talbot had maintained his reputation, Owl members wouldn't have felt compelled to leave the order. If Talbot had invested members' dues in the success of the organization and used the group's funds to actually build a hospital, an old Owls' home, and an orphanage, perhaps the Owls would still be a significant and vibrant national organization today.

The Talbot building, for so long the center of Owl operations, also declined over the years. In its heyday, located close to city hall, fashionable shops, and other heavily occupied office buildings, it was bustling with activity. Over the years the first-floor retail spaces housed a range of small stores, restaurants, and barber shops of ever lower quality. The top-floor offices where Talbot had his exploits were used by a succession of shabby hotels. By the 1960s the building was considered an eyesore, and when it was replaced by a parking garage the local newspaper celebrated the improvement.

Talbot's corrupt leadership was not an indicator of how the Order of Owls manifested in local communities. Undoubtedly, most of the nests that were organized were formed in good faith by members devoted to the stated ideals of the organization: fellowship and the "kingdom of heaven on earth." Activities and entertainment sponsored by Owls were a regular part of life in communities all over the country. News stories and the few surviving issues of the *Owl* indicate that many widows, orphans, and the sick did receive the financial payouts they were promised, and local nests contributed in their communities, even if the national home nest under Talbot did not.

Social events and charitable activities rather than scandals have dominated news coverage of the Owls since Talbot was removed as Supreme Owl, but sporadically, even into the modern era, the Owls made the headlines for the wrong reasons. In one event particularly reminiscent of the Talbot era, in South Carolina in 1961, frustrated Owls were charged with vandalizing the restaurant of a man who had opposed their application for a liquor license: "Chief Strom said that . . . they will be charged with conspiracy to commit house-breaking, grand larceny, vandalism, and safe robbery. 'This was Chicago-type vandalism which we don't plan to tolerate in this state.'"[4] A year later, in Georgia members of an Owl nest were indicted by a federal grand jury for failing to pay taxes on their gambling operation.[5] And as recently as 2015, in Evansville, Indiana, there were accusations of racism when an Owl nest rejected a black applicant.[6] In the arc of the history of the Owls, it is tempting to add these events as the last brushstrokes of an ugly picture. Yet there is no proof that the number of negative activities associated with Owls in the past fifty years is any better or worse than that within other fraternal organizations.

Today many fraternal organizations are still going strong. The Eagles claim eight hundred thousand members across North America, the Elks "nearly a million."[7] The Shriners say they have "thousands of clubs around the world, with hundreds of thousands of members."[8] Although operating on a totally different scale, the Order of Owls still survives, with active organizations in Indiana, Ohio, Pennsylvania, Minnesota, New York, and West Virginia. Individual nest revenues range from a few thousand dollars to several hundred thousand. The headquarters have shifted from East Greenville, Pennsylvania, to West Virginia. It is difficult to find statistics, but there are likely a few thousand members in total. Unlike the days when Talbot supplied the momentum from a strong central authority, the current success of the Owls has been a product of local leadership and resolve. A number of nests still maintain assets valued at hundreds of thousands of dollars.[9] Activities are largely social, such as smokers, dances, and other gatherings. Several nests own and operate their own meeting halls, which they rent out for special events.

Talbot would likely be amazed that the organization he founded in a saloon with his friends still survives over a century later, eighty years after his death.

NINETEEN

—ɯɯ—

TALBOT'S LEGACY

JOHN TALBOT LIVED MOST OF HIS LIFE in the spotlight, slowly but steadily earning a kind of dark celebrity. His activities were covered almost weekly in newspapers from New York to Los Angeles to Walla Walla, Washington, in hundreds if not thousands of articles, often on the front page. Citizens across the U.S. knew John's name and followed his exploits. John reveled in the attention.

Talbot was also the subject or initiator of dozens of lawsuits, leaving a broad paper trail of legal documents not only for his own cases but for those of his clients. For three decades, not a year went by that this lawyer wasn't defending himself in court from charges that included perjury, suborning perjury, fraud, bribery, intimidation, blackmail, forgery, libel, slander, assault, and aiding an escaped criminal. The charge that finally put him behind bars was for white slavery. He ferociously fought off legal challenges to his leadership, questions about his finances, and even, remarkably, questions about his character.

Talbot's character was rightly called into question. He aspired to neither honesty nor integrity. Although John's friends vouched for his honesty (and he needed them to), the record shows he consistently abused the truth. From the time he was a boy, he was always willing to say whatever he thought would achieve his goals. He lied relentlessly in person and in print, claiming a broad range of accomplishments, accolades, and military service to make himself appear successful and heroic. He employed these same tactics in his legal work and to prop up friends in politics and the business world. To support these falsehoods, he published articles and whole magazines under aliases and generated fraudulent letterhead.

In a self-reflective moment (yet writing in the third person), he himself admitted that his character had always been called into question: "His acquaintances say he has since his boyhood been distinguished and remarked for a peculiar egotism and selfishness that in the public mind in his community causes him to be judged a paranoiac by some and a criminal brute by others."[1] His friends framed it differently, granting him a dauntless and admirable desire for success: "John W. Talbot is a hustler, at it day and night with energy and determination that is simply astonishing."[2] Public opinion ultimately sided with his detractors, who said he was "devoid of a decent character ... not simply unclean, but filthy to the very limit."[3]

Talbot was capable of great things, both good and bad. He founded and led a fraternal organization that at its height claimed nearly one million members. From poor beginnings, he amassed assets worth at least half a million dollars (well over six million in today's dollars). He wielded power and influence in the business world and, though he never ran for office, in politics, counting governors and congressmen among his friends. In a time when making the news was about getting a piece of paper into someone's hand, he published work that reached a nationwide audience. We can only imagine how Talbot's influence might have broadened if he had access to the social media tools of today.

The written word was a perfect vehicle for Talbot's agenda. In addition to dozens if not hundreds of magazine articles and newspaper editorials (many uncredited), Talbot published at least five short booklets on a broad range of topics. The first was a defense of his own reputation and character (1909), the second a defense of his mistress's (1916). *Game Laws and Game* dealt with his passion for exotic birds (1917). One, called *Jim Conners* (ca. 1908; no copies remain), ostensibly had as its subject James B. Conners, the national organizer for the railroad Switchman's Union, a figure who received heavy newspaper coverage in the 1900s and 1910s for his organizing tactics. Although all of these give us insight into the mind of John W. Talbot, the work that speaks most directly to his worldview is *Old Maid Ryan* (1910). In it he reveals his fundamental motivation, a vehement rebuke to his working-class roots and the value of hard work. He uses this book to preach that the only true measure of a man is financial success and that the easier it comes the better.

Talbot's failures are equally profound. He lost everything he ever had: his home, his fortune, his family, and the organization he founded. He died destitute and alone. Amazingly, despite his notoriety during his lifetime, Talbot is today forgotten by the community he both terrorized and titillated. Tired of his drama and anxious to feel proud of their industry and harmony, citizens quickly

One of the few remaining traces of Talbot's influence on
the city of South Bend. *Photo by the author.*

let him slip from memory. The only memorial to his existence is a small cluster
of houses along a single block, across from the University of Notre Dame, on a
street he named for himself.

It is not only Talbot who has been forgotten. The tight-knit Irish Catholic
neighborhood that nurtured him as a child and where most of his family lived
out their time has disappeared. The properties along Notre Dame Avenue—the
homes of his mother, his grandparents, his aunt, and his brother, as well as the
site of the Owl "hospital"—are all gone. They have been replaced with student
apartments or redeveloped as large, new single-family houses across what used
to be two or even three residential lots. Little trace of the neighborhood Talbot
knew remains.

John Talbot was a man who lived passionately and made bold choices, trum-
peting his accomplishments but always fearing failure. He aggressively and tirelessly pursued financial success, believing that "you should correct your way of
life or take poison. An unsuccessful man is a curse to himself and a detriment
to his loved ones."[4] His intelligence and charisma helped him develop a cult-
like following of men and women who were willing to do his bidding. He was a
master manipulator without moral restraint who believed that "there are three
ways of getting people to do what you want them to do—Speak kindly to them,

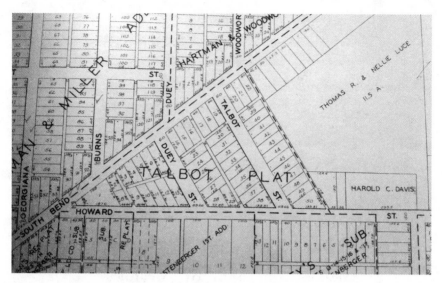

Talbot plat. *Source:* Standard Atlas of St. Joseph County, Indiana
(*Chicago: George A. Ogle, 1895*).

drive them to it, or pound h——l out of them."[5] If he had chosen politics instead
of the law, he may have become president, as was predicted at his birth. Sadly, he
was also likely a psychopath, lacking the ability to show empathy or distinguish
between right and wrong, and he willfully did harm to a great many people.

If we were to look for clues into the mind of John W. Talbot, perhaps the
most telling piece of evidence we would find is the simple Order of Owls motto:

> There's so much bad in the best of us,
> And so much good in the worst of us,
> It hardly behooves any of us,
> To speak ill of the rest of us.

It seems from this that Talbot's greatest fear was being judged. The man had
faced judges and juries again and again, always with a cavalier attitude. The
vast majority of the time, he managed, by whatever means necessary, to avoid a
guilty verdict. Perhaps, despite having walked away from religion years before,
the judgment John W. Talbot feared most was not in this life but the next. Perhaps he knew that he had earned the title of the "devil incarnate."[6]

TWENTY

—⚭—

POSTSCRIPT

MARY OHNESORGE, OWL OFFICER

Mary was the woman closest to Talbot for the longest period of time. She began as Talbot's stenographer but worked her way up to an elevated position in the Owl organization, eventually becoming supreme treasurer, the only female officer of the Owls. She had an office next to his, and he gave her control of the bank account. Over three decades, she was clearly one of his most trusted associates. There is no way to know the exact nature of their relationship, but she was one of the last people to publicly stand by him. She left South Bend around 1931, as Talbot began his final decline.

In 1900, Mary was living with her mother, brother, and older sister in Chicago. Her father had been a member of the Masons, so she was no stranger to men and their secret societies. When her father died in 1891, Mary's sister and brother supported the family. Mary mysteriously appears in South Bend, working for Talbot, in 1910. We don't know what brought Mary to South Bend, but perhaps she went looking for a way to succeed on her own after both her siblings married. She and her mother set up house together about 1909 (they do not appear in the 1908 city directory). By 1914, they had moved into a large wood-frame house at 1010 North Notre Dame Avenue, the property Talbot was promoting as the Owl hospital. The two women lived there together until Mary's mother died in 1919, after which Pearl Spangler, the nurse Talbot hired to give the hospital credibility, became her roommate. Mary appears to have stayed at the 1010 address throughout the Pearl Bagley episode, during Talbot's time in Leavenworth, and until Talbot's ouster from Owl leadership in 1929. After Talbot's personal and professional collapse and the loss of her own position with the Owls, she moved in with her married sister in Allen, Michigan. She died there in 1935.

Her South Bend obituary was brief: "Word has been received here of the death June 10 of Miss Mary Ohnesorge, of Allen, Mich., for many years a resident here. She left here about four years ago. Burial was in Kankakee, Ill."[1] Despite her twenty-five years of service to the organization, there is no mention of the Owls.

PEARL SPANGLER, TALBOT'S ACCOMPLICE

Pearl Spangler was the second child and oldest daughter of Adam Spangler and Mary McIlwaine. Her working-class family lived in Mishawaka, Indiana, a sister city to South Bend. As a young adult, she lost both a brother and a sister to accident and illness. Not long after, at the age of thirty, Pearl eloped to St. Joseph, Michigan, with Edwin E. Smith, a widowed carpenter eighteen years her senior. They married on May 6, 1904.[2] Whatever hopes she had for the marriage, she walked out the door of their home on December 27 of that year, and never went back. By 1905, she was living with her parents and going by her maiden name. Edwin filed for divorce, claiming abandonment, and Talbot handled Pearl's side of the proceedings. The divorce was finalized in April 1908.[3] She met all the criteria for an amorous relationship with Talbot: she was an older but wiser woman with some emotional damage whom Talbot could exploit.

Pearl and Talbot's relationship was facilitated by his son's departure for college in 1915. When Minnie left to be near him, the family home was left unused. Pearl mentions during the Mann Act trial that she lived at Talbot's home while his wife and son were in Bloomington at school. (Leona Mason, an earlier mistress, had also mentioned using the Talbot home when Mrs. Talbot was away.)

When Minnie and John H. returned home after graduation, John had to come up with another plan. Pearl had made a career for herself as a private nurse, and Talbot had for years been laying the groundwork to buy property and create a hospital. In 1919, Talbot hired Pearl to staff this Owl "hospital." As a resident nurse, she would have a place to stay, whether there were patients or not, and could be put on the Owl payroll. She joined Mary Ohnesorge, who had already been living at the property for several years.

This arrangement put Spangler in no position to refuse Talbot's orders. When Pearl Bagley arrived at her doorstop, she acted as a willing accomplice to the woman's horrific treatment. She also fully supported Talbot's defense in court, denying any inappropriate actions on his part and helping to paint an unflattering picture of his accuser. Although Spangler was acquitted, she never appeared to show remorse for her part in the Bagley incident. We can speculate on her motivations. She may have had romantic feelings for Talbot and hoped to please him. She may have taken pleasure in assisting in the abuse. What we know is that Spangler took her place in a long line of people who were groomed over time to serve Talbot and enable him to manipulate and abuse others.

Like many of those people, Pearl Spangler was permanently scarred by her involvement with Talbot. She went back into private nursing when the "hospital" closed and lived out the rest of her life with her sister. She never remarried. She died on May 28, 1938, only a few months after Talbot. Her sister reported that she had become weak and unsteady in her last few years. She suffered a bad fall down her basement stairs and died of shock from her injuries at the age of sixty.[4] The fall was initially considered suspicious and led to a coroner's inquest, but no foul play was discovered. Her last words were reportedly, "I am done for this time."[5]

HELEN BARTLETT, TALBOT'S MISTRESS

Helen was the only woman romantically linked to John Talbot who thrived after their relationship was over, a testament to her strength and resilience. In 1929, hoping to leave the Talbot episode behind her, Helen began looking for options to sell the Jerome Place property in Niles, Michigan. In May the Ancient Order of Gleaners announced plans to build a home for the aged on the site.[6] Success hinged on the city's committing to infrastructure improvements in the area, which it was willing to do. In August a newspaper article claimed that the property had been sold not to the Gleaners but to a Sioux chief, Lawmanin, who claimed Potawatomi roots and "whose forefathers fought and died while laying siege to Fort St. Joseph and other outposts of the white man"[7] within a few blocks of Jerome Place. Lawmanin stated that he would use the property to make a home for a new organization called the Aboriginal Rights and Welfare Society. Neither of these sales appears to have taken place, possibly the result of the stock market crash in October. A 1949 deed shows that Helen ultimately sold the property to Dorothy De Poy.[8]

Jerome Place was not promoted to potential buyers as the perfect family home but as an institutional headquarters, suggesting it had long been used in this way, its amenities more suited to a fraternity rather than a residence. Today an assisted-living facility called Brentwood at Niles operates on a corner of the site. The structures from George Jerome's day are mostly gone, although some of the stonework of the fishponds remains visible. Trees have invaded what had been decorative paths. The chimney from Helen's log cabin can still be seen next to an overgrown trail off the main road.

Helen was a savvy businesswoman and leveraged the assets she gained during her years with Talbot to fund the rest of her life. The public discussion resulting from the Gleaners' interest in Jerome Place nudged the city of Niles to expand its infrastructure into the area south of town. Easement paperwork for power and water utilities show the improvements. After these were available, increasing the value of the land, Helen subdivided the eighty-acre farm property opposite her estate into seventy-two large, wooded lots, many with river frontage. She called the development Brandywine Acres, named for the creek that runs through the area. Over a twenty-year period, she sold off the lots, in some areas selling off the timber beforehand, which both cleared the land for development and made money in the process.[9] She must have retained contacts with fraternal orders, because the International Order of Odd Fellows bought one of these lots and turned it into what is today the Niles Charter Township Park. Although many of the roads through this area today bear the names of early landowners such as Jerome, Beeson, and Decker, Helen and John Talbot are not memorialized in this way. Both Helen and John would likely be amused at the flock of wild turkeys that now roam their former estate.

Helen and her second husband never had children, but she lived out her life surrounded by nieces, nephews, and stepchildren. Known as Aunt Deda, she supported them generously, paying for their college educations. Helen died on September 29, 1951, at the age of sixty-nine, survived by her second husband and three stepchildren. She did not talk about the details of her time with Talbot but kept a scrapbook from the period and a few small mementos of their life together. Her obituary in the *Niles Daily Star* made no mention of either rare birds or John Talbot.[10]

EDITH GREIF, TALBOT'S SISTER-IN-LAW

After suffering the loss of her first husband, Joseph E. Talbot, Edith also lost her second, John Greif, in 1953.[11] Edith was active in the community throughout her life, for years serving as the president of the St. Joseph Hospital Ladies' Aid Society and organizing Circle 572 of the Daughters of Isabella at the Notre Dame Parish. She spent her entire adult life residing on North Notre Dame Avenue. Edith died in 1959, survived by a daughter and a son.[12] Unfazed by the experiences of their father and uncle, both children were involved in the world of law, Dorothy marrying a lawyer and moving to Chicago and Joseph becoming an attorney like his father. The younger Joseph died in an auto accident at the age of fifty-five and is buried, along with his mother, in St. Joseph Valley Memorial Park.

MINNIE TALBOT, TALBOT'S WIFE

Mary and John Talbot were never divorced, although trial records show that she had requested a divorce on at least one occasion. They did live separately at least as early as 1915. She and their son lived in the Main Street house until John H. married and set up his own household. She moved back in with her son and his family in the early 1930s and lived with them to the end of her life. Her business dealings met with marginal success, but there is no evidence that she ever experienced financial hardship. She lived to the age of eighty-seven, a practicing Catholic until the end. Her simple obituary belied the drama of her personal life. It reads in part: "Mrs. Mary Ellen Talbot, 742 S. 23rd St., died in her residence at 11 a.m. Wednesday after three days' illness. She was born in Detroit, Mich., Aug. 4, 1868, and came here from Detroit 59 years ago. Her husband, J. W. Talbot, an attorney, died in 1937. She leaves a son, John H. Talbot, an attorney, of South Bend, and two grandchildren."[13] She and her son are buried in a family plot in St. Joseph Memorial Park, outside the city of South Bend.

JOHN H. TALBOT, TALBOT'S ONLY CHILD

John Harold Talbot developed a legal practice of his own, although his legal career never included his father's theatrics or controversy. Eventually, he endeavored to recover from the drama of his young life. He gave up the national stage, although he dabbled in local politics, serving as a Republican precinct committeeman. He married Edith Mae Smith, and the couple had two children.

Like his father, John Harold Talbot suffered financially when control of the Owls was transferred to Connecticut. While filling in as Supreme Owl for his imprisoned father, he had paid himself a salary and very likely used member dues to support himself, in the model of his father. In 1927, John H. and his wife commissioned architect Callix E. Miller to design and build a stately brick house at 1701 East Wayne Street in the newly developed Sunnymede area of South Bend.[14] It was a neighborhood filled with young professionals, among them the famous Notre Dame football coach Knute Rockne.

But John was unable to escape the effects of his removal from the Owls and the economic hardships of the Great Depression. By 1934, he had lost his house in a foreclosure, and the family moved to a small neighborhood on the east side of South Bend called River Park. The biggest newspaper story of John H.'s later life involved attending the opening of a new neighborhood library.[15] He died on June 15, 1967, at the age of seventy-one at the home of his son. In his obituary, there is no mention of his infamous father or the Order of Owls.[16]

APPENDIX A

Who Is John Talbot?

ORDER OF OWLS

SUPREME OFFICES
SOUTH BEND, INDIANA

HON. JOHN W. TALBOT
Supreme President Order of Owls

Order of Owls

HOW ORGANIZED.

The Order of Owls grew from the frequent meeting of congenial fellows engaged in different lines who had been of mutual assistance. Among them were John W. Talbot, George D. Beroth, J. Lott Losey, Joseph E. Talbot, John J. Johnson, John D. Burke, William Weaver and Frank Dunbar. At one of these informal meetings the methods and teachings of different fraternities were discussed. At this time the suggestion was made to organize an order named the Owls. It was the concensus of opinion the Order should be built along its present lines with the fullest extent of local home rule, and a general governing plan not readily changed.

NO SALARIES.

Those present agreed that in all other fraternal orders, scramble for office and consequent graft were a drawback, and for that reason it was provided that the constitution of the new order should be drawn so that any officer who accepted a supreme office should do so with the understanding that he was amply able to work without salary and to pay his own expenses, and that those who were raised to supreme offices should be raised because of years of service and not by the clamor of hastily assembled bodies, as the result of political intrigue or personal ambition. Three of those present at one of these informal meetings were appointed a committee to work out the plans of the new order. After frequent meetings the present constitution was adopted and the order formally organized at a meeting held in the law offices of Talbot & Talbot, in South Bend, Indiana, November 20, 1904. The plan was the fruit of months of work of the best constitutional lawyers in the Middle West.

GROWTH OF THE ORDER.

The first regular meeting was held in the Hiberian Hall in the City of South Bend, Indiana. The new order immediately went about hiring a hall of its own and when five weeks old opened its first club rooms at 132 North Main Street, in South Bend. These rooms continued to be headquarters for one year, at the end of which the third floor of the Bowman Building, in that city, was leased, and the growing order moved in January, 1907, into a suite of rooms containing a lodge, ante, paraphernalia and buffet rooms, dance hall, kitchen, dining hall and lounging rooms. Since that time extensive stock rooms have been opened for the receiving and shipping of supplies, and a suite of offices have been fitted up for the Supreme Treasurer and Secretary in the same building. The Order was founded in November, 1904. Its second Nest was established in 1905. In June, 1906 it had seven Nests. In June, 1907, it had 68 Nests. In June, 1908, it had 168 Nests; and on December 31, 1908, the membership of the Order was approaching 70,000.

EMBLEMS.

The above is the emblem of the first degree and is protected by U. S. registration and patent. The emblem of the second degree is a large gold disc surmounted by a skull. On the disc appears a coffin and on the coffin is a clown. In front of the disc is suspended the above emblem with the words Honor, Virtue, Loyalty. On the back of the disc is found the number of the degree. The emblem of the third degree is the same as the second, except that the number 2 on the back and front is changed to 3 and the charm is embellished with a diamond, which is emblematic of the degree. The fourth degree emblem is the same as the second and third, except the number 2 of the second degree is changed to 4, an eye takes the place of the skull from which the disc is suspended, and a pyramid is added.

HOME RULE.

The constitution of the Order gives each nest the greatest possible degree of home rule. Each nest fixes its rate of dues, provides its own benefits, fixes its own black ball rule, makes its own provision for a quorum, provides its own age of eligibility, and in almost all respects, without interference from the supreme officers or other nests, manages its own affairs. In this order it is not possible for officious politicians at the supreme office or from subordinate nests to assemble and regulate the affairs of any nest of the Order.

SUPREME ORGANIZATION.

That fraternal societies succeed is usually due to their inherent worth rather than their management. Those whose experience fits them for power are selected for railroad, insurance companies and manufacturers by a small board of directors composed of men conversant with the requirements of the business and the abilities of the employees, and not by all stockholders, creditors, customers and employees assembled in a hall. Public control is a failure when compared with honest private business management. *Why should a man who don't understand anything about it have a right to decide who shall control a great institution that others have built?* In any organization when popular vote annually controls, it is impossible to enlist good organizers because they can't be assured of a position beyond the end of the year. The result is no organizer can be found working for the Eagles or Elks who has been with them more than two years, while in the Standard Oil Company there is a pension department and the Pennsylvania Railroad Company has employees who have been with it more than thirty years. THERE ARE TWO METHODS OF GOVERN-MENT, THE POLITICAL AND THE BUSINESS METHODS. THE POLITICAL METHOD MEANS GRAFT, DISHONESTY, INCOMPE-TENCE. THE BUSINESS METHOD MEANS ABILITY, CONTINUITY OF POLICY AND HONESTY. THE OWLS CHOSE THE BUSINESS METHOD. That having been determined, it was proposed that, as in Scottish Rite Masonry, the executive officers be elected for life, but this plan was rejected because a man when elected to office, may, at the time of his election, meet every requirement, but subsequently may become lazy and indifferent, or insane and incompetent, and it would be impossible to remove such if his tenure was for life. On that account, it was agreed the selection of officers should occur annually so that incompetence and dishonesty could be avoided. In some respects the plan of government follows closely upon Scottish Rite Masonry, while in others the plan of control more resembles Odd Fellowship.

DEGREES.

Men die or resign, consequently it was certain the positions of the founders of the order would become vacant, also that others must be chosen to fill the vacancies in the Home Nest. To choose these men at random, because of good looks, hand shaking ability, or their own ambitions, would end as do chance results generally. IN BUSINESS ENTERPRISES PROMOTIONS ARE MADE BY THE MEN AT THE TOP WHO KNOW THE BUSINESS AND ITS EMPLOYEES, AND BEGINNERS ARE NOT JUMPED, FROM THE FRONT DOOR, ON THEIR FIRST ENTRANCE, TO THE PRESI-DENCY OF THE COMPANY. THEY ARE TRIED THROUGH SUC-CESSIVE STEPS UNTIL, NOT THEY, BUT THE INSTITUTION ITSELF, FEELS THAT THEY SHOULD BE PLACED IN CHARGE. So in the OWLS, there are four degrees. The first degree of the order is given to all initiates. This degree furnishes the secret work for subordinate Nests. The number of persons who may take this degree is unlimited, and is consequently very numerous. Among the many who take it are found some whose entry to the Order was brought about by personal ambition or a desire for profit. It is impossible in taking men into an order, to determine whether they come in with a view of building up the order, or of helping themselves at the expense of others. But if they have entered and taken this first degree in Owldom, they soon begin to show their real characteristics and principles, and this enables those who are in charge of the order's affairs, and those who have been pro-moted to different degrees above the first, to judge of the fitness of promotion and advisability of promoting to higher degrees those who have taken the first degree. To the second, third and fourth degrees, there can be no application made. The second degree is given to those whose services to the order have been so great as to merit advancement. Those who take the second degree are selected by the members who have already earned promotions in the order. Those who take the third degree are promoted from the second, and the fourth from the third. It is due to this system that this order has been kept free from in-fluences of fraternal politicians, and that in its management, graft is unknown. The second degree can be had by only 150 living persons, and but ten persons can be admitted to the degree in any one year. It is usually conferred at the time of the Home Nest's annual meeting. Those in the second degree who merit further advancement are rewarded by having the third degree conferred on them. The third degree can be had by only fifty living persons. From the third degree are chosen those advanced to places in the Home Nest, the entry to which requires the taking of the fourth degree. The degrees in Owldom increase in beauty as they progress. But their nature is so sacredly guarded that only by treading the way of progressive promotions in the order, can they be learned. It can safely be asserted that the ritual of the order is the most beautiful and impressive that has ever been written.

COMPENSATION OF OFFICERS.

In all business enterprises and most fraternities it is customary to pay salaries to officials, but it is in religious movements that the most earnest and enthusiastic workers are secured and the greatest success has been obtained; and in the most successful religious organizations men work without salaries and are prompted solely by their love of the cause. If salaries are paid in an order and its officers are elected by delegates, it results always in political strife and fights by men who selfishly seek personal profit. If salaries to officers should be paid by those in authority, it would result in those officials some day promoting men because they wished to favor them with the profits instead of serving the order. It would also keep men from resigning offices which they could not fill with justice to the order. Every person who accepts an office in this order does so with the understanding that he can afford to perform the duties of his office without financial reward.

AIMS.

It is the plan of the Order to use its revenues whenever they exceed its expenses, in building and maintaining three great benevolent institutions. The first of these is intended to be a home and school for the orphan children of Owls. The second is intended to be a home for aged and infirm members of the Order. The third institution planned is to be a general hospital conducted upon the most modern scientific lines. This last institution is intended to make possible the giving of the best medical and surgical attention and care in difficult and capital cases to all members of the Order, either at a minimum expense, or at no expense at all. It is believed the building of such institutions will do more good for mankind than would the payment of salaries and the furnishing of positions from time to time to ambitious men.

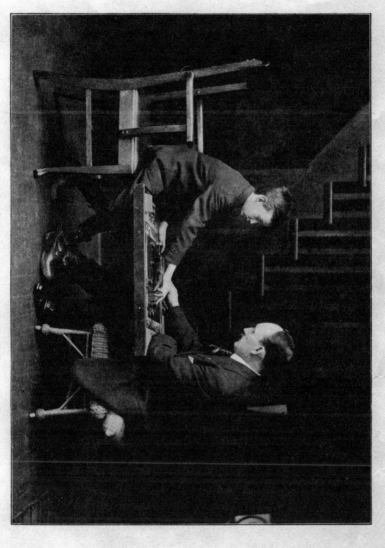

John W. Talbot and his son John H. Talbot

HON. JOHN W. TALBOT

The guiding star of the Order on its successful career has been its present Supreme President. Consequently all the calumny and vituperation that malice, envy or ambition could prompt against any man has been directed against him.

If you wish to learn a man you must know him personally and intimately. If you can't do that you must try to learn of him, and the way to do that, is to ascertain what he is, from those who do know him. KNOWING A MAN AND BEING ACQUAINTED WITH HIM ARE DIFFERENT THINGS. A LITTLE MAN MAY BECOME ACQUAINTED WITH A BIG MAN BUT HE CAN NEVER KNOW HIM, FOR TO KNOW A BIG MAN, YOU MUST BE A BIG MAN. Heresay is not evidence therefore when some one who does not know a man, or is too little to understand him, tells you of him, it is well to pass such opinions unheeded. We are asked so frequently "who is John W. Talbot?" that we decided to pick from the big men of the city where he lives some big men who knew him and to have them answer in their own way this pointed question. No one qualified to answer would say that our subject was a perfect man, that he had no faults, that he was always pleasant to meet or had no enemies. Everybody who knows this man Talbot realizes he can make enemies and that he does, also that he can make friends. There is this about both—the enemies and friends—are positive in their charters—the enemies will never compromise their enmity while the friends are partizans of unreasoning zeal. Both will tell you, if they are just, that the man Talbot never took a dishonest dollar, never broke a promise, never betrayed a confidence, never repudiated a debt or followed an enemy after he was down. He strikes quick and fights hard. He don't ask quarter and don't squeal. There may be many better horsemen, sprinters, boxers, shots, orators, lawyers, thinkers, students and moralists than he but he can take a place well up with any of them. He is nearly forty years of age, the son of a tailor and tailoress who trace their ancestry to the druids. He had few early advantages of educational character and no powerful influences to aid him but he is now, through his own efforts, exceedingly well educated and his pro-

John W. Talbot and his famous saddler Gopher

fessional success is a subject of envy. He is reputed to be a man of considerable means. He is about five feet nine inches tall, weighs in ordinary street dress about 155 pounds, is a little bald in front, has good eyes, good teeth, smiles well, wears a dark moustache, has altogether very good features and seems sometimes to talk without speaking. His habits are athletic and moral. He does not use tobacco, drugs or liquors in any form. He is married and has a son now growing up. For the rest we will let the personal letters of others speak. The men asked for these letters are men who stand so high in the atmosphere of success as to need no introduction once their identity is disclosed.

The first letter is presented to you in typewritten form as well as in facsimile. It was written by Hon. Timothy E. Howard who is now dean of the law department of the University of Notre Dame. Mr. Howard has been a member of the Indiana state senate also the chief justice of the Indiana Supreme Court. He is a man of national scientific and literary reputation and among Catholic educators has no superiors in ability or esteem. His letter will be found interesting.

The second letter is written by the present post-master of South Bend who was appointed, not because he was a politician, but because he was fit to handle a great trust. He differs politically from Mr. Talbot. Hon. Cadmus Crabill is a personage unique and striking; a writer of wonderful ability, a man of high moral character who has few if any enemies and a host of friends. No man can describe the charm of his character and the standing of any man is established where he is known, by his endorsement.

Hon. Joseph Neff is the president of a bank in South Bend and is not only a financier but a lawyer of ability. He is a cool and calculating man of affairs who measures men very carefully and does not incline to enthusiasm. The individual who would attempt to deceive Mr. Neff would probably land in jail. He has had ample opportunities of judging our subject and the result, is in his letter, which is itself a literary treat.

Theodore Thorward is a Baptist divine who retired from the ministry at the call of large business interests to take charge of the affairs of the independent telephone companies of Indiana. His exceptional ability has made the lines he rules the strongest in his state. He is a big man and you will note that in his letter which follows he addresses himself to the traits of character it was his privilege to observe in Mr. Talbot.

Hon. Earl R. Perrin is at the present time the highest officer in the state of Indiana in the Uniform Rank of the I. O. O. F. Mr. Perrin is a clean cut, energetic man of affairs. He is South Bend's leading broker and has won his way in Odd Fellowship, as do all officers in that Order, by force of merit. Fifteen years ago he was an ordinary advertising sign painter. Today he is known as a man of wealth and influence, and is easily recognized as one of the leading men of Indiana. We append a letter from him which will be read with interest.

United States Post Office

SOUTH BEND, INDIANA

" Who is JOHN W. TALBOT ? "

A hale fellow well met- one who is a great friend
to a friend and a bitter enemy to an enemy. He is one
who finds in books a solace and a satisfaction- in
nature a source of joy and inspiration and in the hearts
of friends a comfort and a prompter of high hopes and
ideals. He knows law and he knows life. He knows
books and he knows men. He knows the beauty of flowers,
of sunrises and sunsets and, too, he knows the beauty of
living, of loving and aspiring- John W. Talbot is this
and more and those who know him best think more.

Cadmus Crabll

P. M.

South Bend, Indiana, March 24, 1909.

Mr. William A. Jackson.

Dear Sir:—You ask me the question, "Who is John W. Talbot." Mr. Talbot is a gentleman whom I have known all his life. He was born in this city, in the same ward in which I have resided during the whole period of his childhood, boyhood, and manhood. He is a self made man in the best sense in which that term is used, having risen from the position of a poor boy to his present standing as a successful man. After completing his education he studied law and entered upon the active practice of his profession. He was successful almost from the beginning, and those in Court, whether litigants, counsel or citizens had no occasion to ask, who is John W. Talbot. But even more remarkable has been his success in the establishment of the Order of Owls. The growth of this young, vigorous organization has been phenomenal, and though the work of organization has been aided by his many capable associates, it can truthfully be said that the chief source of the success of the Owls has been the vigorous and resourceful genius of Mr. Talbot. I trust this answer may be sufficient answer to your incisive question.

Yours very truly,

T. E. HOWARD.

TIMOTHY E. HOWARD
LAW OFFICE
222-24 JEFFERSON BLDG
SOUTH BEND INDIANA

March 24, 1909.

Mr. William A. Jackson,

Dear Sir—

You ask me the question, Who is John W. Talbott? Mr. Talbott is a gentleman whom I have known all his life. He was born in this City, in the same ward in which I have resided during the whole period of his childhood, boyhood & manhood. He is self-made in the best sense in which that term is used, having risen from the condition of a poor boy to his present standing as a successful man. After completing his education, he studied law & entered upon the active practice of his profession. He was successful almost from the beginning, & those in court, whether litigants, counsel or citizens, had no occasion to ask, Who is John W. Talbott. But even more remarkable has been his success in the establishment of the "Order of Owls." The growth of this young & vigorous organization has been phenomenal, & though the work of organization has been aided by his many capable associates, it can truthfully be said that the chief source of the success of the Order has been the vigorous & resourceful genius of Mr. Talbott. I trust this answer may be a sufficient answer to your incisive question. Very truly yours, T. E. Howard

March
25th
1909.

The question, "who is John Talbot?" is not an easy
one to answer. Unlike other human beings he is not
susceptible of classification. You cannot put a
label or a tag on John Talbot. He does not do what
he does because some other fellow has done it or because it has become a custom to do it. Precedents
are not very important in the eyes of John Talbot.

He is a lawyer by profession. He is very successful
in his profession. As a man of affairs he has been
unusually successful. This is proven by the fact
that he is supposed to have accumulated quite a fortune, and is further proven by the fact that he has
been the originator and the inspiring spirit in the
organization and development of the Fraternal Order
of Owls, which has in the short space of four or five
years drawn together into its membership a great many
thousand human beings.

He is a philosopher and literary genius as all will
testify who have been readers of his publication
"The Owl." He is an artist in the sense that he has
a fine appreciation of the beautiful, and knows how
to get the best results from a camera.

His credit is good. He meets his obligations
promptly.

He has enemies, as every man has who is a doer of
things. He also has friends. Friends who are men
of good standing and who have known him for years and
are familiar with his character.

Very truly,

PATRONIZE HOME PHONE AND USE INDEPENDENT TOLL LINES

6000 HOME PHONES IN ST JOSEPH CO

HOME TELEPHONE COMPANY

MAIN OFFICE AND EXCHANGE
212 AND 214 WEST COLFAX AVENUE

THEODORE THORWARD, PRES.
H. G. MILLER, FIRST V. PRES
H. B. STALEY, SECOND V PRES
B. F. HARRIS, TREASURER
E. R. STOLL, SEC'Y & ASS'T TREAS
W. I. PATTON, AUDITOR

South Bend, Indiana. Mar 29, 1909

"Who is John W. Talbot?"

In answer to the above question I will change the same to
"What is John W. Talbot?"

John W. Talbot is a hustler, at it day and night with
energy and determination that is simply astonishing.

When you see him hustling and commanding you think he
must have forgotten Rule No. 5 of the Order of Owls, " Don't
take yourself to --- seriously."

He is a friend not only in need, but at all times one
that you can bank on; a friend that you always know where
to find.

These two qualifications make up John W. Talbot to me.

Thos. Thorward

THE SOUTH BEND HOME TELEPHONE CO.

Headquarters
DEPARTMENT OF INDIANA
Patriarchs Militant, I. O. O. F.

MAJ. GEN'L. EARL R. PERRIN
Department Commander
LIEUT. COL. GEO. W. FREYERMUTH
Asst. Adjt. Gen.

South Bend, Indiana, April 12th, 1909.

Mr. George D. Beroth,

South Bend, Indiana.

My dear Sir:- Replying.to your inquiry of recent date as to who
John W. Talbot is, will say that from an acquaintance of twelve
or fourteen years, I have learned that he is a lawyer of unusual
ability, a scholar and a true friend to those who are worthy of
his friendship. A man of unquestioned executive ability, he has
accomplished in the fraternal field a feat not of the ordinary
kind in that he has made the Order of Owls, in the few short
years of its existence a society to be recognized and respected.
His departure from the usual methods of launching a new organization has, in my humble opinion, been the most important factor
in his success. He has had many critics, but what successful
man has not? They have served a purpose, and it was to polish
the rough gem and bring forth its beauty and value. I never knew
a man who was as ready to welcome criticism, and I never knew one
who was more benefitted by it. Criticism does not always mean
"to correct" error, but as frequently means the enlightenment of
the critic, and so it has many times been in the case of Mr.
Talbot and his critics. As a lawyer his fame is wide-spread.
As a scholar his work shows his worth. As a friend, he is gen-
erous to a fault and never failing, a watch that beats true for
all time, and never runs down.

In my acquaintance I have not met a man who is as well
qualified to direct the affairs of such a society as the Order of
Owls, with its aims and purposes, as is John W. Talbot.

Sincerely and fraternally yours,

Earl R. Perrin

HON. JOS. E. TALBOT, General Counsel

JOHN J. JOHNSON
Supreme Invocator

B. J. CRAMER
Supreme Past President

GEO. D. BEROTH,
Supreme Sec'y.

J. LOTT LOSEY
Supreme Treas.

DR. C. B. CRUMPACKER, S. V. P.

APPENDIX B

The Character and Life of John W. Talbot,
Exposed by an Outraged Woman

THE

CHARACTER AND LIFE

OF

JOHN W. TALBOT

SUPREME PRESIDENT ORDER OF OWLS

EXPOSED

BY

AN OUTRAGED WOMAN

ONE OF HIS VICTIMS

WHO IS JOHN W. TALBOT?

And the Awful Story of How He Ruined My Life—By One of His Victims.

MRS. LEONA MASON

John W. Talbot is having a pamphlet widely distributed for the purpose of telling the people what a wonderful man there is among us. This pamphlet is being put out in the name of the Order of Owls and gives a number of letters which the circular says were written by business and professional men answering the question, "Who is John W. Talbot?"

That pamphlet was printed and sent to the Owls quite a while ago, but observe that it was not distributed in South Bend until after the published accounts of a woman's attempt to shoot Talbot, down by the City Hall.

So many things, both kind and unkind, have been said to me and about me with reference to John W. Talbot and so much has been said about the newspaper reports that a woman shot at him, and so many things have been left unsaid in the press reports of that affair, or have been said in such a way as to mislead the public with regard to the facts; all of which has tended, and was intended to do me personal injury, that I have concluded to print and publish my own account of the events which led up to that unpleasant occurrence and to answer in my own way the question, "Who is John W. Talbot?"

If you do not believe my story, it will not be me who will censure you. Had anyone six years ago given me such a history as I am now about to write, I certainly would have branded it as a falsehood; this, however, shall not deter me from giving the plain truth, and I am certain that the telling of it will not and cannot blacken me more in your estimation, than has the untruthful and misleading statements that have already been published.

My story shall be just the plain truth, let that hit whomsoever it will, as bad as the truth is I shall not make excuse for my life and actions in associating with John W. Talbot. For such conduct there is no excuse, other than that he made love to me, and caught me in his web, and I must suffer the consequences. It may not soften your criticism of me any, but personally, it is a great satisfaction for me (in view of the shadow that is over my life) to know that ever since my association with Talbot the police have carefully watched my house, and make report that they have never seen a man, save John W. Talbot, enter there, whom they had reason to believe was there for any other than the most lawful and respectable purpose. And I say to you now, that the police are correct in making that report to the department, and as strange as it may seem, I can say truthfully that John W. Talbot was never a welcome guest at that house, although he did frequently come there. This is a queer kind of consolation, but John W. Talbot has done so many things to drag me down that I am glad of the police report or for any kind of proof of the fact that I am not what Talbot has tried to make me out to be.

This story is not being told to arouse your sympathy; I am not telling it to you because of innocence and virtue upon my part; I am not telling it because I am entirely free from fault, but I am telling it because John W. Talbot has ruined my life, and has shamefully and cruelly treated me, and like the villian that he is, has lied about me to further blacken my character; and has by the most relentless system of persecution, tried to force me back to a life of shame with him. John W. Talbot knows I am not what he says that I am; he knows that I am

2

struggling with all my energy to free myself from him, for my own sake, for the sake of my honored family name, for the sake of my dear, true sisters, and for the sake of my little daughter, and to inform and warn men and women and innocent girls who may not know the brute; to warn good citizens of and from this criminal of all criminals, I relate this true story.

I do not forget my unfortunate position; nor must I forget that in my effort I have had the loyal support, the real help, and the earnest sympathy of some of the best and truest of friends. My own good sisters have always been loyal and true; but aside from these, some of the purest, whitest souls whom God ever recognized as His own, have opened their hearts and their homes to me, and have faithfully stood-by me and suffered persecution from Talbot, that I might have a fair chance.

Having said this, I now say again that this letter is not issued to arouse your sympathy, but to let the world know something of the true character of the villian who has come into my life, the villian, John W. Talbot, self-styled and self-appointed, Supreme President of the Order of Owls. *There are others who know of his criminal life, but they dare not expose him.* If there are those who know more than I do, let them come forth and say so; but while we wait I shall impart some things I know of this devil incarnate. Of course, you are saying: If I want to tell my story, why don't I wait and tell it in Court? Nothing will give me greater satisfaction than to tell my story in Court when the time comes, if it ever does come, but it is my belief that the time will not come. When Talbot and his attorneys saw what was coming Talbot refused to face me and I went from the Police Court without being allowed to testify, and who knows what will happen next? When those honorable gentlemen (his attorneys), who were getting some of John W. Talbot's dirty money to assist the state in a pretense at prosecuting me, saw that I would tell my story to the Court and likewise was anxious to put Talbot on the stand, they kept the facts from the people by resorting to a trick of the law, in dismissing the case, and then filing a new complaint in the Circuit Court, where, without previous notice to me, I was put under $5,000 bond to answer for trial next fall, and if I am alive I will be there when wanted.

As to the story of the shooting, I shall say little; but will, before I finish this article, give you the sworn statement of two of the State's witnesses against me; that of Humane Officer Abraham Moore, of the

3

police force, and that of George D. Beroth, Supreme Secretary of the Order of Owls. The latter is a friend and intimate associate of John W. Talbot's, and their testimony will inform you as to how and what happened, as they saw it.

Several months ago John W. Talbot, seeing that the facts of his bad character and criminal life were becoming generally known, and that the Owls from all over the country were writing here for information about him, conceived of a plan to stop these reports. He wrote up a lot of letters very complimentary to himself under the title, "Who is John W. Talbot?" Then sent his office girl and other persons about the city to ask business and professional men to sign them. A few of these men signed the letters as they were; several wrote, instead, some verbiage that meant nothing, while others who were brave enough, did not sign them.

A few of these letters are printed in a pamphlet prepared by John W. Talbot himself, entitled "Order of Owls, Supreme Offices, South Bend, Ind." This is the pamphlet that was first sent to the Owls, and later was distributed over the City of South Bend. When you read these letters please note that all criminals were born somewhere, all of them love the fresh air, most of them are successful in their *line,* but none of them have a good character; and mark you, *not one of these letters say that John W. Talbot is a man of good character.*

Here is what this conceited pup, this vile character, says of himself; I quote his own language:

"HON. JOHN W. TALBOT.

"The guiding star of the Order on its successful career has been its present Supreme President. Consequently all the calumny and vituperation that malice, envy or ambition could prompt against any man has been directed against him.

"If you wish to learn a man you must know him, personally and intimately. If you can't do that you must try to learn of him, and the way to do that is to ascertain what he is from those who do know him. KNOWING A MAN AND BEING ACQUAINTED WITH HIM ARE DIFFERENT THINGS. A LITTLE MAN MAY BECOME ACQUAINTED WITH A BIG MAN BUT CAN NEVER KNOW HIM, FOR TO KNOW A BIG MAN YOU MUST BE A BIG MAN.

4

"Hearsay is not evidence; therefore, when someone who does not know a man, or is too little to understand him, tells you of him, it is well to pass such opinions unheeded. We are asked so frequently, 'Who is John W. Talbot?' that we decided to pick from the big men of the city where he lives, some big men who know him, and to have them answer in their own way this pointed question.

"No one qualified to answer would say that our subject was a perfect man, that he had no faults, that he was always pleasant to meet or had no enemies. Everybody who knows this man, Talbot, realizes he can make enemies and that he does; also that he can make friends. There is this about both—the enemies and friends are positive in their characters—the enemies will never compromise their enmity while the friends are partizans of unreasoning zeal. Both will·tell you, if they are just, that the man Talbot never took a dishonest dollar, never broke a promise, never betrayed a confidence, never repudiated a debt or followed an enemy after he was down. He strikes quick and fights hard. He don't ask quarter and don't squeal. There may·be many better horsemen, sprinters, boxers, shots, orators, lawyers, thinkers, students and moralists than he, but he can take a place well up with any of them.

"He is nearly forty years of age, the son of a tailor and tailoress who trace their ancestry to the Druids. He had few early advantages of educational character and no powerful influences to aid him, but he is now, through his own efforts, exceedingly well educated and his professional success is a subject of envy. He is reputed to be a man of considerable means. He is about five feet nine inches tall, weighs in ordinary street dress about 155 pounds, is a little bald in front, has good eyes, good teeth, smiles well, wears a dark moustache, has altogether very good features, and seems sometimes to talk without speaking. His habits are athletic and moral. He does not use tobacco, drugs or liquors in any form. He is married and has a son growing up. For the rest we will let the personal letters of others speak. The men asked for these letters are men who stand so high in the atmosphere of success as to need no introduction once their identity is disclosed."

Now, isn't that nice? It's delightfully refreshing to have one say such very smart things about himself! Talbot has a lot more complimentary letters that he wrote in his own office and sent his office girl about the city to have business and professional men sign. Read the letters for yourself, then interview the men and see if I have not

5

told you the truth. John will give you a copy of the pamphlet if you do not have one; he is always pleased to have people read the flattering things he says of himself.

John told me that the Owls over the country look upon him as being as big a man as the President of the United States. Here is the conceited old bird upon his perch in his finest feathers. What do you think he looks like?

Now have a good look at THE BIG OWL ON HIS NEST!

HON. JOHN W. TALBOT

The Supreme President of the Order of Owls in the full regalia of its fourth degree. This is considered a remarkable piece of work in velvet, satin, silk, lace and gold.

The above is from a Post Card which the pretty bird is distributing so freely.

"Who is John W. Talbot?" is his own question, and he answers by saying that he is "Hon. John W. Talbot." I have known him very well for six years, having been with him a good deal, too much, I am sorry to say, and I have heard many, very many people speak of him as being dishonorable and criminal, but never until he himself wrote it did I hear anyone speak of or refer to him as being honorable.

He says "TO KNOW A BIG MAN YOU MUST BE A BIG MAN." We farmer girls used to take delight in seeing a toad sit upon a clod and blow himself full of wind, then open his eyes big to see if anyone was looking. Well, I am not a BIG MAN, but I am a woman who, unfortunately, has been SMALL enough to know much of this self-styled "BIG MAN," and as a woman who knows him well, yes, too well, I know he does not tell the truth when he says *That the man, Talbot, never took a dishonest dollar, never broke a promise, never betrayed a confidence or followed an enemy after he [she] was down."*

I know that he lies when he tells you that *"His habits are moral."* When he says that *"He does not use 'drugs or liquors in any form'"* he simply states what I know to be an absolute untruth. John W. Talbot

6

is not only a drunkard, but he is a dope fiend of the worst kind. Talk about morals and good habits. John W. Talbot does not know what decent morals and good habits are. If to associate with lewd women and licentious men, with thieves, robbers and degenerates is moral, then he is a moral man. If to fill up on liquor, get drunk, curse and swear and befoul a woman's carpets in his helpless condition, is not to use liquors in any form, then Talbot tells the truth; but before you believe either of us, inquire of the neighbors who know (I will furnish you their names), then see the empty liquor bottles which John W. Talbot has left in my cellar and on my premises as evidence of his drinking habits.

On the first page of that wonderfully self-complimentary circular which he distributed so liberally, you will find this statement: *"The ORDER OF OWLS grew from the frequent meeting of congenial fellows engaged in different lines."* Observe that he does not say occupations or professions, but *"lines,"* and adds *"who have been of mutual assistance."* Look over the list of men whose names are given there; inquire who they are; then ask yourself if (with the possible exception of one or two) you would like to invite them to your home of an evening that they might get acquainted with your wife or daughter, or with your son or your husband. So much for John W. Talbot's account of himself.

"Who is John W. Talbot?" He was a licensed lawyer six years ago when I got my divorce, and he was a smart lawyer too, *i. e.,* he knew every trick of the profession, but he is not practicing law now; he is under disbarment from the practice because he procured Rose Duck as a false witness in the La Porte Circuit Court. (See Court record in State *vs.* Duck.) Some time ago, in Talbot's office, I got hold of an album which contains a picture of this same Rose Duck, photographed sitting upon the arm of a hall-tree exactly like the one in Talbot & Talbot's office. In this picture Rose wears no other apparel than her hair hanging loosely over her shoulder. John W. Talbot seems to have a mania for the nude and for licentious pictures. In this same album are a lot more of the vilest things that have ever been photographed. Several of them have been taken in the most indecent positions imaginable and the big Morris chair John W. Talbot has in his office is a favorite background.

Yes, my picture is in that album, and before I get through with this story you shall know who took it, how it was taken, where it was taken

7

and how it got there; but I wish to tell you some other things before I do that. I want first to answer the question, "Who is John W. Talbot?"

He is the vilest sinner, the deepest dyed criminal, the most heartless, cruel wretch who ever led a woman astray. When I consulted him as an attorney, he acted square, treated me right, and was perfectly lovely as I supposed—that is the way he gets people—I was a green country woman in trouble, my husband and I were mis-mated, and could not agree. I wanted a divorce and Talbot got it for me. There was another lawyer in the case, to whom I had first gone, and he wanted to overcharge me. I did not know what to do; some one suggested that I see Talbot, and I did. This slick devil sympathized with me; helped me out of my difficulty, got my confidence, threw his charm about me (like a spider or a snake gets its victims), lied to me about himself, about his wife, and about his family relations; deceived me into believing that he was about to obtain a divorce, said he lived very unhappy and longed for a companion who was agreeable; made arduous love to me; spent his money freely to show me a good time and took me to the theatre and to many other places of amusement. I had never until then had such attentions shown me. These experiences were new to me. I was dazed by their charms and I was blinded by their glitter. Talbot knew he had me in his net; then he took me to Chicago to a theatre. I trusted him, and before I knew it—well you know my fate. It is not necessary to tell you that from that time on I was his victim; he had me in his grasp, and he kept me there until a few months ago, when I took courage, sent my little girl away to school, ordered Talbot out of my house, broke up my home, packed my furniture, and got away from him. But the end is not yet; he is constantly on my track or in my path, he haunts me and torments me by day and night. Why did I not tear myself away from him long ago? That question is easier to ask than it is to answer. You, who ask that question do not know of what you are speaking, neither do you know the villian. I awoke to my folly, but I was in his clutches. Like a fly in a spider's web, or a child under the deadly charm of a serpent, I saw no way of escape. He often said to me: "There are three ways of getting people to do what you want them to do—Speak kindly to them, drive them to it, or pound h—l out of them." He has made use of all three methods with me, but I will not do as he bids, neither will I go back to him, now that I am free.

Did you read in the papers about the time that he tried to kill me (I mean the time when Esther Graffenberger, his former office girl, sued him for assault and battery and for damages, after he had knocked her down and burned her hat and scarf in my stove because she interrupted and would not let him choke me to death)? No, you did not read of it in the papers, at all, for it was never published, not a word of it, although the filing of the complaint was public and the whole thing is spread upon the records in Justice Morris' court, South Bend, Ind., just as it came to him in a most sensational complaint—a very newsy document, setting out all the facts, and the papers have at all times had access to these records. The newspapers of South Bend are either afraid to publish anything about John W. Talbot, or they are unwilling to soil their sheets with his filth. It may be that the Owl printing is too valuable to lose; anyway, they never publish the vile things that Talbot does. They didn't even tell about it when a woman shot him through the coat, the bullet grazing his body, or when another fired four shots at him. When Esther Graffenberger filed that complaint John W. Talbot never so much as denied it, but paid her $25.00 damages and offered her $100 if she would get certain information for him, relative to myself, and afterwards took her back again into his employ. Since the papers did not tell you about that occurrence, I will.

About 11 o'clock on the last night of February (if I am mistaken about the day the police record will clear that up) Esther had just gone up to her room. I had not yet retired for the night when who should enter the house, unannounced and unexpected, but John W. Talbot, and he was in a rage. He flew at me and said: "D—n you, I came to kill you, and I'm going to do it now." He took from the rack that stood by the door, Esther's long fur scarf and quickly wound it about my neck and began choking me. I screamed for help and Esther came running down stairs. When she opened the stair door Talbot saw her, and, leaving me, ran to her and struck her, knocking her backward into the stairway. Then he came at me again and said: "D—n you, I told you I came to kill you, and am going to do it now." As he spoke he struck me in my face and broke my nose. I ran, bleeding, into the street and called for help. The neighbors telephoned for the police and they came to the house in the patrol. Talbot escaped, but, before going, put Esther's hat and blood-stained scarf into the fire. When things quieted down the doctor was called and dressed my nose

9

and a policeman kept guard for the night. Then Esther's suit for damages and the subsequent settlement. Before this suit for damages was settled Esther carried a gun and declared that she would shoot Talbot.

"Who is John W. Talbot?" He is the man who took me with him on a trip to Michigan, stopped at Detroit and Jackson, and while at the prison there (as he afterwards told me) made arrangements for the escape of his friends, Slater, Spellman and Allison.

"Who is John W. Talbot?" If you will take the trouble to read the confession of "Yock Allison," which is in the hands of the Board of Pardons, at Lansing, Mich., and by the making of which Allison obtained his pardon, you will find, he says that on the night of their escape from prison, one of these three men had keys to all of the doors, and that they reached the outside of the prison easily, and that they came direct to South Bend and sent for John W. Talbot; that Talbot received them, provided them with food and shelter, gave them citizens' clothing with which to escape, money to spend and guns with which to defend themselves. While I am telling of these criminals I might say that John W. Talbot, himself, showed me the place where these men were in hiding just as Allison tells it, and that in the confession of Allison he mentions not only the Big Owl but several of the smaller Owls whom the Supreme President designates in his pamphlet as *"Congenial fellows engaged in different lines who had been of mutual assistance."*

Yes, he has the nerve to print his name "Honorable John W. Talbot," but before trusting him it would pay the men and women who are strangers to this nasty bird in robe of velvet, satin, silk, lace and gold, who sits watching his prey, to pay a visit to South Bend, Ind., the home town of the "Big Owl," and there learn from the people who know him (except a few of his henchmen) who will say that he is the shrewd rascal of the night, to be trusted by none, and to be shunned and feared by all.

"Who is John W. Talbot?" He is the center, the brains and the controlling spirit of the biggest gang of thieves, robbers, cutthroats, blackmailers and buncosteerers that have ever preyed upon the people. When Slater, the noted crook, was shot by an officer in Ohio, Talbot greatly mourned his loss and said to me, "He was the best fellow of the lot." He said, "If only I had not arranged for him escape from the prison he would not have been killed."

Who disposed of the silk stolen, some years ago, from the B. & O. R. R. Co.? The testimony in that case shows that beyond question it was John W. Talbot, and the record shows that he was acquitted only upon a mere technical error in the indictment. For proof see record of case of State vs. Talbot, in Circuit Court, Marshall county.

Who was it planned the deal by which my father was buncoed out of $5,000.00 and sent both him and mother to an early grave because of the incidents and trouble that followed? I know that John W. Talbot had a hand in the arrangements by which Red Austin was let go. I was with him in Chicago when he met Austin's friend, Chimelle, and put that deal through. I was in darkness then, but I know now what the meetings of those criminals meant.

Who helped the state to prosecute the Springborn buncosteerers and let the crook, Foster, get away? John W. Talbot was a very zealous representative of the people in the police court that morning assisting his brother, the prosecuting attorney. It was John W. Talbot's personal friend, Brady, of Chicago, who took Foster out the back way and escaped, while the Talbots waited for another warrant to be sworn out in the Circuit Court and be placed in the hands of the sheriff, and any person knows that the police present could have arrested Foster on the spot had Talbots instructed them to do so.

Who was it that blackmailed Mr. Lewis, the woolen mill man? John W. Talbot told me that his share was $4,000 and Kate McCullum got $6,000. In this connection John said that Kate was the only woman he ever knew who would do things right.

Who was it that was disbarred from the practice of law because he got his friend, Rose Duck, to testify falsely in the La Porte Circuit Court? John W. Talbot.

Who was it that tried to fix the jury in the Joseph E. Talbot disbarment case? The Commissioners told the Disbarment Commissioner that it was John W. Talbot. And who was it that said to me that the judge who tried that case was such a good friend of his that there was no danger as to the outcome of the trial? John W. Talbot.

Who was it, that one day in his office, showed me a big roll of postage stamps and said they were worth $1,800 and told me they are easy? John W. Talbot. That was after the big robbery of the Chicago postoffice and before the stamp thieves visited the South Bend postoffice—plenty of time elapsed for the "Big Owl" to run out of stamps.

11

It was John W. Talbot who, at another time, when I was about to enter his private office, told me not to do so, saying that Webb (the man who recently went to the penitentiary for killing the sheriff of Pulaski county) and the boys are in there counting stamps. And John told me not to look in there or they might blow my d—d head off.

Who was the "BIG MAN" *whose "habits are athletic and moral,"* who *"strikes quick and fights hard,"* that one night came up by the side of a man not much more than half his size, and, without warning, struck him in the face and then ran away, like any coward would? Ask the Supreme Vice-President of the Owls, Dr. Crumpacker, who was with him, if it was not John W. Talbot.

Who was it that wrote a silly, soft letter to Mr. Lampbert, signed my name to it, mailed it to him from Chicago, adressed it to his residence in such a style that his wife would be certain to open it, and afterwards sent Mrs. Lampbert one of those awful pictures of me, and wrote across the face of it that I was her husband's sweetheart? The writing is in the hand of John W. Talbot and I have the letter, also the picture.

Who was it that afterwards, to carry out his villainous plan, first visited Mrs. Lampbert, herself, then sent a dirty henchman of his, a two-cent Mishawaka lawyer, Isaac Kane Parks, to urge her to sue me for damages and alienation of her husband's affections? John W. Talbot.

Who sent this woman souvenir postcards from Providence, R. I., called upon her, and personally urged her to take legal action against me; tried every way to have her bring the suit, said he would see the matter through court for her, assured her that she would get money out of me, offered to pay all costs of the suit, and finally offered her $5,000 if she would get me out of the way? John W. Talbot.

"Who is John W. Talbot?" He is the dirty thief and low-down blackguard whom (one afternoon when we were all down town) the neighbors saw enter the house and home of the lady with whom I roomed. When we returned that evening I found much of my wearing apparel gone, and in the center of the lady's front room we found an earthen vessel, which this dirty, low thing, who styles himself "A BIG MAN," had used for nature's convenience, and let stand there as evidence of his lack of appreciation of all things decent. I might add, that the lady's brother-in-law, who lives next door, ordered Talbot ("THE BIG MAN"), in a very positive way, to return

12

the things he had taken from that house. And without further notice they were returned at once and were left on the porch, where we found them.

"Who is John W. Talbot?" He is the man who sent me a check for $24.00 to pay for the twenty-nine (29) window lights that were broken out of my house this spring, the night after I moved out. When the police came upon the villain who did that job, he escaped, but left his horse tied in the alley and it proved to be John W. Talbot's "famous saddler," Gopher, shown in John's pamphlet.

"Who is John W. Talbot?" He is the man who ordered a friend of mine not to allow me to use the automatic telephone at his place of business. This man did not obey Talbot's orders, but continued to allow me to use his 'phone, and, strange to say, several nights later the window lights at his place of business were broken in the same manner as mine had been on the night when Talbot's horse was found tied in the alley by my house.

"Who is John W. Talbot?" He is the man who takes delight in tormenting my friends, as he thinks, by calling them up at night to answer the telephone. Talbot has an automatic 'phone and ringer. With this he awakens the household by keeping the 'phone ringing for indefinitely long periods of time. Of course, it takes a "BIG MAN" to do such a noble, inspiring thing.

"Who is John W. Talbot?" He is the personal friend and business associate of Madge Cole, the female with whom he may be seen horseback riding on the streets of South Bend most any time, and with whom he is in partnership in the owning and managing of one of the well-known houses of prostitution of South Bend, Ind., and the inmates of which he obtained a number of unmentionable graphs of themselves that he displayed in "his album of choice forms." This he tells, in his own hand, under the pictures—I the album.

"Who is John W. Talbot?" Who was it tried to sell the Red Front resort, on Colfax Avenue, in South Bend, to an Elkhart man, Mrs. Cripe, and pledged her immunity from prosecution, while his brother was State's Attorney?

Who was it that a little later had his office girl swear out a warrant for the arrest of this same woman, then acted for the state, in prosecuting her for keeping a rooming-house on Michigan Street, one in which the *"greatest constitutional lawyers of the middle west"* had no financial interest?

Who was it that afterwards (when charges were filed against his brother) induced Madge Cole, a South Bend prostitute (Talbot's partner in business), who had a roll of money at the time, to take Mrs. Cripe to Chicago so that she could not testify against these great "Constitutional Lawyers" and tell how the "BIG MAN" had tried to insult her, how he had escorted her from the attic to the basement of the Colefax Avenue joint, showed her the book account of illegal beer sales, the contents of the slot machine, the various rooms and the receipts from each inmate; and said he had guarantees in the way of protection? Any member of the Disbarment Committee will tell you that, not only this woman, but also the friend who was with her, when they looked the house over together, told them, under oath, that it was John W. Talbot.

"Who is John W. Talbot?" He is the conceited dog who calls himself "Hon. John W. Talbot," and for whom the people who know him have such contempt that almost everybody regretted the poor marksmanship of the woman, whom the papers say shot at him with intent to kill. There would have been more condemnation of her, and more sympathy expressed for the brute, I know, had she shot a worthless, yellow dog. People are saying, "She ought to be fined for not hitting him." "It's a pity she missed him." One man said, "I suppose he was so d—d crooked she couldn't hit him." A real nice gentleman, who used to be a farmer, said: "She ought to have put a bullet through the old Owl and tacked his carcass to the barn door, as farmers often do." The owl, you know, is a natural thief, a chicken thief, and people hate it and like to shoot at it. Another man said: "He is so black no one could see him; no wonder she missed him." A good man said to her: "Woman, don't do such a thing again; don't shoot at him any more; don't do it, I say, but get yourself a good gun, go to the woods and practice, and learn to hold your weapon steadily."

Who said such things? Not the few men of the town, who do disreputable things, dress well, wear bland smiles and fly around at night with the BIG OWL. No, not these; but the best people in the city. Even the ministers of the Gospel expressed regrets that the woman was not a better shot.

14

"Who is John W. Talbot?" He is the big-eyed bird of prey who originated the Lodge of Owls as a self-serving agency, appointed himself Supreme President and some of his henchmen *"who have been of mutual assistance"* as the other Supreme officers. He is the man who fixed the constitution so that it would be hard to depose him. He is the man who holds this lodge (the Order of Owls) in such high respect that at a social session, a little more than a year ago, he provided an entertainment for his local nest of nasty birds, in the form of a dance, a real nice dance, and the females present were not the good wives and sister of these birds of prey. Oh, no, these dear women were at home looking after the babies or dreaming dreams of future happy homes, while the inmates from several well-known houses of prostitution were, at the invitation of the Supreme President, dancing with their husbands and brothers. (See testimony of Geo. Comstock and Joseph Calvert, two of these round-eyed night fowls, who were summoned before the Disbarment Committee of the St. Joseph County Court.) The testimony of these fellows will also show, that upon another occasion, the Supreme President gave evidence of his *"athletic and moral"* habits by introducing to the feathered tribe assembled, a Chicago woman, who gave a fancy dance before the male members, and who, according to a prearranged plan, lost all of her clothing and danced in the nude before them, to the great delight of the Supreme President and the disgust of others.

"Who is John W. Talbot?" He is the man who desires to create in the minds of those who do not know him the impression that he is an honorable man of family. He is the man who says (in his pamphlet) that he is married and has a son growing up. He is the man who took me to a meeting of the Owls in Davenport, Ia., and introduced me as his wife, to Mr. and Mrs. Finger, Mr. and Mrs. Benedict, and to the other big OWLS; and who took me to Traverse City, Mich., to Niagara Falls, to Buffalo, N. Y., and to other places and introduced me to his Owl friends as his wife.

"Who is John W. Talbot?" He is the dirty villain who is doing his best to further ruin me socially and financially, and he is the thing who has been tormenting me, and trying, by all manner of means, to convince my friends that I am a bad woman. He says that he wants me to come and live with him and that he will torment me until I do. Well, I'll die first! Talbot has the negative of a most disgraceful picture of me, the picture to which I have heretofore referred, and

15

he has sent prints of that picture to every person whom he thought he could influence against me. He wants my friends to turn me out, but they have not done so. He has pasted that picture upon the windows of people's houses, has sent it to men and to women whom I do not know, has sent it to the people in the neighborhood where I lived with a lady friend, and has sent copies of it to this friend herself and pasted it upon the porch post of her house, and has sent it to her friends with notes telling them of my bad character. John W. Talbot put this picture of me in his album with the licentious pictures of well-known prostitutes and disreputable characters, and wrote not only my name under it, but wrote the vilest sentiments in the album about me, and passed it around among his office help, and among his friends; showed it to both girls and men, and this is the picture I promised to tell you about.

That picture was taken away back in July, 1905, four years ago, in Mr. Talbot's own house on North Main Street, South Bend, and the taking of that picture has set every fibre of my body on fire with hatred for John W. Talbot. I know you will not believe me, nobody can understand it, but I will tell you the truth about it, and it is the truth when I say that six years ago I employed John W. Talbot to secure a divorce for me. He did not charge me anything at all for his services; but that employment has cost me what money cannot buy— it has cost me my good name and has heaped shame upon the name of my family and upon the name of my little girl.

After my divorce had been granted by the court, Talbot began making ardent love to me, and he was very nice about it, indeed. Yes, I knew he was a married man, but he told me that he and his wife were having serious trouble, and that he was about to get a divorce from her. He assured me that there was no question about the divorce. I was a green country girl and I thought what he told me was true. He would show me a nice time, take me to the theatre, and spend his money lavishly upon me. He took me to Chicago, to Detroit and to many other places. His kind treatment of me continued for some time, until I finally realized my mistake and tried to get away from him—then our trouble began. That was four years ago. One day in July, 1905, I was out with some friends spending the day and he saw me. That evening he met me down town and induced me to go with him to his office. Nothing unusual happened until he got me there; then he locked and bolted the door, drew down the shades,

16

turned on the light (he was in hot temper), and said: "I saw you today with Mr. ——, and I'll fix you that you will never be seen again in the company of another man. D—n you, undress yourself right here before me or I'll kill you." I feared him, but I refused to do his bidding; what followed was awful, such cursing and damning and such conduct as took place there cannot be described, when, from exhaustion, I was unable to longer resist him, he took his knife and cut and tore from my body every stitch of clothing, save only my shoes and stockings; then he put my clothing into a satchel and carried it out of the room, telling me that if I made an outcry that he would kill me; and his conduct was such that I thought he would kill me. He securely fastened the door on the outside and I did not see him again for several hours, during which time I was confined within his inner office room with no clothing with which to dress myself, and fearing to call for help lest he would kill me. About midnight he returned to the room, in a terrible rage, and brought with him a suit of his own clothing, and with oaths and curses and with a gun, forced me to dress myself in his clothing and accompany him on the street and to his own home several blocks from his office. At the Cummings building I clung to an iron railing until he wrenched me from it and forced me along with him. Mrs. Talbot was away from home at the time, and in his own house he kept me for three days and three nights, a prisoner, without food and without any clothing but a loose bathrobe, because I would not do as he desired. Why did I not call for help? I simply could not. Put yourself in my position, then ask yourself the question. I had been deceiving my parents and my friends as to my relations with Talbot. I was not without fault, and I could not bring myself to the point of exposing my double life, though I died in torment. It was at this time, in his own house, that John W. Talbot, after he had nearly starved me, took a gun and threatened to kill me if I would not allow him to take my picture nude. The expression upon my face in that picture should convince anyone of the terror I felt, as he pointed his gun at me and made me submit while he took that picture; and now that coward and criminal of the deepest dye is showing that obscene picture to everybody, both men and women, as proof that I am a bad woman. I know I have done wrong; I was wronged by that black devil, and now he will not let me alone, but insists upon tormenting me by a system of persecution. I have done wrong in other things, but not in the taking of that picture.

17

HERE ARE TWO PICTURES OF ME.

The large photograph was taken last spring. The small one was cut from a nude picture that John W. Talbot recently pasted on a lady's house, on the side nearest the street, where passers-by could see it. I want the people to know about that picture. I want you to see the disheveled hair and the distressed look upon my face. I want you to answer for yourself, if that untidy hair and that haggard look, are the expression and pose of a woman who was doing an act like this willingly, or who was having a picture taken to please herself or any other person.

18

"Who is John W. Talbot?" In conclusion, from what I know and have already said, John W. Talbot is a most peculiar type of man who has many accomplishments and some few good traits of character. He is always busy, works hard, pays cash, generally fulfills his promises, dispenses with a liberal hand and seldom fails to get men and women under obligations to him; he is an apparent friend and sticks close to those whom he can use and will do and dare for them; but he is a relentless foe of those who cross his path; and for these reasons he is universally despised and feared by honest men and virtuous women. With this statement I conclude my awful story, and let his witnesses tell the rest.

Following is the evidence of Abraham Moore of the Police Force and of George D. Beroth, Supreme Secretary of the Order of the Owls, which I promised to give you:

STATE OF INDIANA, } ss.
ST. JOSEPH COUNTY }

In the South Bend Police Court before I. S. Romig, Special Judge, State of Indiana vs. Leona Mason, assault with intent. Appearing for the State, Cyrus E. Pattee, William McInerny, Miller Guy. Appearing for the defendant, Charles A. Davey, Daniel Pyle.

ABRAHAM MOORE, a witness produced by the State, after being duly sworn, testifies as follows:

DIRECT EXAMINATION BY CYRUS E. PATTEE.

Q. State your name to the Court.

A. Abraham Moore.

Q. What business are you in, Mr. Moore?

A. I am a Humane Officer for the City of South Bend and do police duties around this office.

Q. Were you near the station on the 21st day of June, day before yesterday?

A. I was.

Q. You may state whether or not you hear any shooting at that time.

A. I did.

19

Q. State what you saw defendant do, if anything.

A. Well, I was at the police barn, patrol barn, and just as I was coming out the door I heard a shot fired. It sounded like a shot, but I first thought it was a firecracker that the boys were shooting off; then I heard a revolver shot and I started toward Main Street, and just as I started that way Talbot came running along and said, "Stop that woman; she will kill me."

Q. Who said that?

TALBOT ON THE RUN
20

A.   John W. Talbot.   And of course I went on that way and seen two shots fired—defendant fired two shots—two shots struck the ground and the second I heard whistle as it went past me.   I went right on and told the defendant to stop shooting, and I got there just about the time she fired the last shot.   There were three shots that I heard and seen discharged.

Q.   Where was John W. Talbot?

A.   Well, I cannot tell you—he was going on past me the last I saw of him.

Q.   What position did Mr. Talbot occupy with reference to the defendant, Mrs. Mason?

A.   Well, as I said, the last I saw of him he was passing me; I was coming this way and he was going that way (indicating).

Q.   Did you see the pistol in the hands of the defendant?

A.   I did.

Q.   Which way in reference to John Talbot was that aimed?

A.   It was aimed in an easterly direction.   In the direction Talbot was going.

Q.   What did you see on the ground?

A.   Grass and gravel struck up and some fire from a revolver.

Q.   Where was that, Mr. Moore?

A.   It was right opposite, the first two that struck the ground as near as I can say, they struck the ground between myself and the one who discharged the revolver.

Q.   When that took place, what did you do?

A.   I went to the defendant, but before I got there I called to her to stop shooting and, of course, I went to her and just laid my hand on her arm and grabbed for the revolver.   She naturally dropped the gun and——

Q.   Did you pick up the gun?

21

A. I did.

Q. What did she say?

A. I don't know as she said anything.

Q. What did you do with the defendant?

A. I took her to the station and turned her over to the proper officers.

GEORGE BEROTH, a witness produced by the State, after being duly sworn, testified as follows:

Q. State your name to the Court.

A. George Beroth.

Q. What is your business?

A. Real estate and Fire Insurance.

Q. Mr. Beroth, were you in your office on or about the 28th or 29th of February, 1909?

A. I think I was.

Q. Do you remember of seeing the defendant, Mrs. Mason, about the building about that time?

A. Yes, sir.

Q. Where did you see her?

A. I saw her on the stairway going to the street.

Q. You may state to the Court what you saw Mrs. Mason do?

A. I saw her have a revolver.

Q. Where was she standing?

A. She was standing on one the first few steps leading down to the street.

Q. How far were you from her?

A. I was about two steps from my office door standing against the railing. I heard the shot and ran out.

Q. How many shots did she fire there?

A. I am sure she fired three shots.

22

Q. Do you know in what direction she fired those shots?

A. She fired the shots in the direction of the entrance door to the Talbot office.

Q. Did you, after the shooting, notice any place where the shots struck?

A. I did; yes.

Q. You may tell the Court where they struck.

A. The glass in the door was broken and I saw where a bullet hole was plugged up with putty in the door casing.

Q. Did you see any evidence as to any of the shots having struck any person?

A. I did not.

Q. Do you know where John W. Talbot was at that time?

A. John W. Talbot was standing in the hallway.

Q. What, if anything, did you hear Mrs. Mason say at that time with reference to the shooting regarding intent or purpose?

A. She, when I first saw her, said: "Beroth, I'll get that black devil."

Q. Was that before or after she shot?

A. That was before.

Q. Did she say anything else that you remember?

A. After the shooting she says, "I'll kill him yet."

Q. Did you know to whom she referred?

A. Why, I took it that she referred to John W. Talbot.

CROSS EXAMINATION BY MR. DAVEY.

Q. Did you say your business was that of a Real Estate man?

A. Yes, sir.

Q. And what else?

A. I don't know as I have any other business for a livelihood.

23

Q. Will you say that you have not?

A. I will say that I am in no other business for the purpose of making a livelihood.

Q. Have you any business that you are following for pleasure?

A. I am Supreme Secretary of the Order of Owls.

Q. You and Mr. John W. Talbot are associated closely and confidently in business, aren't you?

A. Only so far as our duty as officers demands.

Q. You have been associated in that connection ever since the order was founded, haven't you?

A. Yes.

Q. You was one of the founders?

A. Yes.

Q. Mr. Talbot was one of the founders?

A. Yes.

Q. Mr. Joe Talbot is General Counsel for the same organization?

A. Yes.

Q. How did you happen to be in such close proximity to Mrs. Mason at the time you referred to?

A. I thought I heard a shot fired in the hall and stepped out and closed my office door as she had started down the stairs.

Q. Did you mean that you thought you heard a revolver?

A. I was sure that I heard an explosion of some kind of firearms in the hall.

Q. Had you any idea when you stepped out what you were going to see?

A. None at all.

Q. Then you did not suspect when you left your office and went into the hall that Mrs. Mason might be there and that she might have caused the report that you heard?

24

A.   I didn't think of that at all; that wasn't in my mind.

Q.   Had it been in your mind that Mrs. Mason might come up there and do shooting?

A.   Yes.

Q.   What had led you to believe that?

A.   Because I had been told that she had attempted to shoot Talbot before.

Q.   When?

A.   I cannot tell you when, but some time previous to this.

Q.   Witness, did you see John Talbot at the time that you referred to?

A.   Certainly I saw him.

Q.   Where was he?

A.   He was standing in the hallway at the head of the stairs.

Q.   She was there?

A.   She was a few steps down the stairway.

Q.   Then when she shot towards the door you spoke of in your previous examinations, she wasn't shooting toward the iron post which he was behind?

A.   No, because he left.

Q.   He had gone away from there?

A.   Yes, he left there.

Q.   Did she shoot up the stairway all of the time he was behind the post?

A.   She didn't shoot until he left his position behind the post.

Q.   When you first saw Mr. Talbot he was behind the iron post?

A.   When I first saw him he opened the office door quickly and stepped out into the hall and took a position behind the post.

Q.   Did he say anything?

A.   Yes, he said, "Stop that," or something like that.

Q. What did she say?

A. I don't remember that she said anything.

Q. Where was he when she had the revolver in her hand?

A. Where was he?

Q. Yes?

A. Behind the post.

Q. Where was she?

A. She had started down the stairs.

Q. Did she come up stairs again?

A. She did not; I think she just turned on the steps.

Q. Then tell the Court whether there is a railing, an enclosed railing, between the stairway and the door of the Talbot office.

A. There is.

Q. Tell the Court how it was that she could, from that position, shoot into his front doorway?

A. As near as I could judge, by raising her arm just a little bit above horizontal it would bring the point of her revolver just above that railing.

Q. Was there any other place that you supposed a bullet struck?

A. There was another place that I supposed, but I don't know.

Q. Where was that?

A. I think Mrs. Mason shot in the direction of the front office door.

Q. Now, when Mrs. Mason was shooting in the directions that you have outlined, did you see Mr. Talbot standing in either of the doors?

A. No.

Q. You don't know where in the office Mr. Talbot was, do you?

A. He wasn't very far behind the door.

Q. What was done then, after this incident; what happened;

what was done?

A. By whom?

Q. By anybody?

A. Well, Mrs. Mason (I observed her probably more closely than anyone else), she went down the steps and I judged she was putting the revolver in a handbag, and the doors swung on her and I was alone in the hall.

Q. Did it appear to you, Mr. Beroth, that Mrs. Mason, at that time, was not shooting directly at anybody that was visible to.her. It appeared to you at that time that way, didn't it?

A. It appeared to me that the first two shots that she fired that she was trying to get John Talbot.

Q. He wasn't in sight, was he?

A. He was going through the door.

Q. Did the bullet strike Mr. Talbot?

A. Not that I know of.

Q. You would have known it if it had, wouldn't you?

A. I think I would.

Q. You saw Mr. Talbot when he was going through the door. I suppose he was going rapidly, wasn't he?

A. I saw Mr. Talbot with his hand on the doorknob. He was crouching.

Q. You could not see both hands or see whether he had anything in his hands?

A. No.

Q. Did you follow him to see whether he had anything in his hands?

A. No.

Q. He was crouching. Just from where she stood, she couldn't tell from her position just what he was attempting to do, could she?

A. He was going through the door in a stooped position.

Q. What do you mean by going through the door in a stooped position; you mean crouching?

A. Exactly.

Q. A moving crouching?

A. Yes.

STATE OF INDIANA, }
                  } ss.
ST. JOSEPH COUNTY }

I, Mary D. Walworth, do hereby certify that I took down in shorthand the testimony of the several witnesses, to-wit: Abraham Moore and George Beroth, at the hearing had before Iden S. Romig, Special Judge in the case of the State of Indiana vs. Leona Mason, held in the City Police Court in the City of South Bend, Ind., on the 23d day of June, 1909, and I hereby further certify that the above and foregoing is a true transcript of the testimony of the said several witnesses as transcribed by me from my shorthand notes of such evidence made at the time.   MARY D. WALWORTH.

STATEMENT.

As to the truth of the facts given in this article, I made solemn oath before the Clerk of the Court.

I have carefully verified the statements which have been told me by others, and the information I give is from the most reliable sources.

In most cases I have avoided using the names of individuals other than John W. Talbot, but can give them if necessary.

Having done this, I leave you to judge if I have done my duty and the people a service in warning the public as to the character and influence of John W. Talbot, a most dangerous man.

                                        LEONA MASON.
General Delivery, South Bend, Ind.

28

STATE OF INDIANA, }
ST. JOSEPH COUNTY. } ss.

I, Leona Mason, having been first duly sworn, say upon my oath, that the statements and facts in this article contained and given as by me, and as of my personal knowledge, are true, and that the statements and facts as given to me by others I believe to be true and are true to the best of my knowledge and belief.

LEONA MASON.

Subscribed and sworn to before me, this 30th day of August, 1909.

FRANK P. CHRISTOPH,

Clerk of St. Joseph Circuit Court.

Seal of the St. Joseph
Circuit Court, Indiana.

COPIES OF THIS PAMPHLET
CAN BE SECURED BY
ADDRESSING
LEONA MASON,
GENERAL DELIVERY,
SOUTH BEND, INDIANA.

THE END

APPENDIX C

The Question

·PUBLISHED MONTHLY BY THE·
·QUESTION CO·INDIANAPOLIS IND·
(SAMPLE PAGES)

HELEN BARTLETT

THE QUESTION

Published by the Question Publishing Company.

Vol. 12	Indianapolis, Indiana, December 1, 1917	No. 12

This is the 127th of our issues, each of which is given exclusively to one subject. Extra copies not sold.

BRUTALLY ATTACKS SISTER.

SUBJECT OF CRIMINAL OR INSANE PROCEEDINGS

ECCENTRIC—EGOTISTICAL—CRIMINAL—INSANE

ATTACKED SISTER BECAUSE SHE MOVED CHICKEN HOUSE

ATTEMPTED TO BITE OFF MAN'S FINGER

MANY NEIGHBORS PRONOUNCE HIM INSANELY SELFISH

ARGUES WITH HIRED MAN ABOUT PAY

Helen Bartlett, the celebrated ornithologist, game raiser and lecturer on game propagation, has removed her game farming business from Cassopolis, Michigan. Miss Bartlett has been compelled to make this move by a series of mysterious persecutions and injuries suffered by her in her business at Cassopolis during a period of ten years.

Miss Bartlett's location has been upon a farm about five miles from the town of Cassopolis, county seat of Cass County, Michigan. This location has been isolated, removed from police and official protection and ideally situated for a game farm, but also very favorably situated for any person so evil minded as to desire to injure Helen Bartlett or her stock.

More than ten years since, Ralph W. Hain, who lives in a cottage located at Diamond Lake, six miles distant from the farm where Helen Bartlett's business has been located, began a series of petty persecutions, annoyances, and interferences with her from which he has never desisted. Hain is a man past fifty years of age who was formerly in the railway mail service but who was dropped out of that service years ago without any explanation being made to the public. Helen Bartlett relates that several years ago Hain began his persecutions by going to her home in her absence, forcing himself into her bedroom, searching her effects, opening her mail and reading her letters. She says that he later, upon her return to her home, proceeded to read to her in the presence of her old mother and father letters written to her by her personal friends, which he had purloined, and that in their presence he announced that he intended to control her, dictate her conduct, govern her, and select her friends; and that he would not allow her to wear or own clothing or adornments that he thought more valuable or attractive than his wife's.

Since that time the Bartlett place has been the subject of secret visits at night by persons unseen and she has suffered damage to the extent of thousands of dollars as the result of these visits.

At one time Helen Bartlett imported from the headwaters of the Amazon in South America a pair of Curassows at an original cost to her of three hundred dollars and a shipping charge of more than four hundred dollars. The birds were delivered to her and within a month after having been placed upon her farm they were so tame that they were liberated by her and permitted the freedom of the place. They were so attached to her that when she went upon the lawn of her place they would follow her about, eat out of her hand and call to her to attract her attention. The birds were as large as ordinary turkeys and her handling of them attracted the attention of ornithologists from all parts of North America. Ralph Hain came uninvited to the place, saw the birds, noted their attachment to her, and her manner of handling them, and went away. The next day one of the birds died. An examination of its intestines revealed crushed glass. A few weeks later the other bird was missed. A search was immediately made for it and the bird was found to have had its feet destroyed. As a result, it died.

Miss Bartlett is a profound student of biology and has developed and bred a fur-bearing rabbit of large size, the skin of which when tanned is stronger and tougher than buckskin and the fur of which is superior to muskrat. The result of her experiments in this regard have attracted general attention. She placed in a breeding pen the best speciments of her breeding stock of these rabbits. They attracted many people who came in automobiles to examine them until an afternoon when Ralph Hain again came uninvited to her home. The second night thereafter all the rabbits died. An autopsy revealed phosphoric poisoning.

On one occasion Helen Bartlett found valuable pheasants on her place that had been poisoned and on other occasions she found valuable birds that had been killed, in some cases chopped to pieces and in others giving evidence of having been tortured. On other occasions she found sheep lying dead, mysteriously killed, at another time a watch dog, a beautiful white collie, was poisoned. Dr. Gookin, the bacteriologist of Epworth Hospital in South Bend, Indiana, analyzed the intestines of the collie and determined the death to be from phosphoric poisoning. The collie had been a favorite of Miss Bartlett, followed her everywhere and was attached to her so much that it undoubtedly caused jealousy or aroused hatred. The day before the collie died, Ralph Hain visited the Bartlett place. Immediately after the death of the collie she called the attention of the county authorities to the circumstances and the newspapers of Cass County gave it publicity. Although she did not state her suspicions as to the source of the poison, she then received an anonymous letter stating that the poisoning was done by one Jack Whitmore, a tenant on the farm of Ralph Hain, adjoining the farm on which she con-

ducted her business. Later another letter was received anonymously, stating
that one Frank Taylor, who lived upon the Jewel place immediately north,
had helped Jack Whitmore do the poisoning. Whitmore and Taylor are men
of exceptionally kind disposition. Both have always been very friendly to
Helen Bartlett and have on numerous occasions assisted her and placed her
under obligations to them by their kindness. Whitmore has since left the
Ralph Hain farm dissatisfied with Hain, and Taylor is said to have had difficulty in collecting the wages due him for work done for Hain. The anonymous letters accusing Whitmore and Taylor were in the opinion of Helen
Bartlett, sent to her with the intention of causing her to quarrel with Whitmore and Taylor. She is certain that neither Whitmore nor Taylor were connected in any manner with the poisoning of her pets or injury to her property.

Ralph Hain has a son and a daughter. The daughter is married and resides at Elkhart, Ind. At one time a letter written to Helen Bartlett and duly
and regularly mailed to her was obtained before its delivery to her by the
daughter of Ralph Hain and unlawfully opened and its contents made known,
and Ralph Hain discussed the contents of that letter obtained and unlawfully
opened and written by his daughter. Later Hain appeared at the Bartlett
home and brought a woman with him and introduced her as Mrs. Nancy
Hain. He said she had married his son and she had graduated from an oste-
opth school in Kirkwood, Mo., and he intended to locate her at Cassopolis
and drive out all the doctors because they were fakers. Later this Nancy
Hain attempted to practice in Cassopolis and opened an office in a building
there but in a few weeks she disappeared. Most of the anonymous letters
received by Helen Bartlett have been postmarked at Elkhart, Ind., where
his daughter resides, and at Sedalia, Mo., where his son is said to be living.
Miss Bartlett says that Hain has gone about the county talking about her
and slandering her and unjustly alleging that she is guilty of immoral offenses and otherwise wrongfully attempting to injure her in the opinion of
the community.

The people of Cass County have been very much interested in Helen
Bartlett's work and it is a common thing to see from ten to fifteen automobiles, on a Sunday, at her place, filled with sightseers, attracted by her industry. The Cass County papers have been for years filled with accounts of her
activities and successes but immediately after each issue of the paper, she
has always suffered loss and received anonymous letters. Several times
Ralph Hain has been to her place in her absence and following such occasions she claims that correspondents from which she had received letters per-
taining to her business and whose letters she left lying upon her desk where
Hain or other visitors could inspect them, if so contemptibly minded, have
received letters slandering her and threatening them and her with harm.
Finally she concluded that her safety could only be secured by locating in a
city where she could have police protection and she purchased a very beautiful place within the limits of the city of Niles, a place formerly owned by a
state game commissioner of the state of Michigan, and she proceeded to move
her business and property to her new place. In the operation of moving the
property it became necessary to have transported a chicken house and
she engaged a Mr. McIntyre of Cassopolis to do the moving. In this operation Mr. McIntyre was assisted by the help of the Bartlett place. Ralph Hain
was evidently on watch and when the men had proceeded out of hearing and
out of sight with the building and nobody appeared to be home but Helen
Bartlett, Ralph Hain drove into the yard in a Ford car and rushed into the

house. Finding her in the kitchen he proceeded to attack her. A visitor, who, unknown to Hain, was in the house at the time rushed to her assistance and the visitor with her assistance managed to hold Hain, although during the operation he foamed at the mouth and attempted to bite off and did seriously bite the finger of the visitor. Later when he was thought to have quieted down and before anybody could intervene, he brutally struck her, after which he rushed away. He threatened as he went that she would be killed and he would injure any person who came to her assistance and that Brother Jim was going to sue her.

Helen Bartlett has consulted the celebrated legal firm of Hendryx and Mosier of Dowagiac, Michigan, and in the event that Hain's wife or other friends do not restrain him he will be punished criminally if he is sane, or placed in the state asylum if insane. His sanity has long been doubted. Insanity has in other instances affected the family. Hain's bother died a year ago in the state asylum at Kalamazoo.

Hain's eccentricity causes him to hate all young men who surpass his own son. He also hates the doctors of Cass County because his son's wife failed in Cassopolis as an osteopath. He claims he controls the Sheriff, Judge of Probate, Prosecuting Attorney and other County officials. He says he drove Charles Kimmerlee out of politics, says he handles the Governor. He spends much time forcing himself on institutes, public bodies and meetings and imagines he can sing, play the flute, and is an orator. He married early a woman whose maiden name was Eva Spaulding, whose relations with Hain's father, mother, brothers and sister are said to have ever since been unfriendly, so much so that a colored girl who worked for him states that his wife threatened to leave him because he gave some peaches to the wife of his brother Jim.

The second oldest child of the family, Grant Hain, died in the Michigan asylum three years since and the oldest child, Ralph W. Hain, has been a subject of remark and amazement for the past ten years. His acquaintances says he has since his boyhood been distinguished and remarked for a peculiar egotism and selfishness that in the public mind in his community causes him to be judged a paranoiac by some and a criminal brute by others. Some contend that Hain has all his life been like the brother who died in the asylum. Others believe he has been secretly drinking too much hard cider and this has caused him to brood over his non-success in life, which, together with his wife's demands and jealousy of Helen Bartlett and the failure of his two children, is accountable for his conduct. Some of his neighbors think he is simply of criminal character and belongs in Jackson prison. This latter theory is borne out by his assertions that he owns Eby and Des Voignes and controls the prosecutor and that he made Charley Kimmerlee eat mud. Many believe Hain to be a shrewd, clever criminal who should be incarcerated for the best interests of the community.

An interesting sidelight is thrown upon Hain by the fact that he allows his brother Will to work for and help his mother at great expense and inconvenience while he always finds excuses for refusing to help her. When she had limestone on a car at Dailey and needed the use of his team he compelled her to let it be thrown off on the ground and to later haul it herself. He took her manure spreader from her for the use of his tenant and deprived her of it. He contracted with his own tenant to pay 15 cents per meal whenever it was necessary for him to be at his own farm, which adjoins his mother's, but the tenant says Hain often failed to take or pay for such meals because he could go to his mother's and sponge his meals.

CURASSOWS

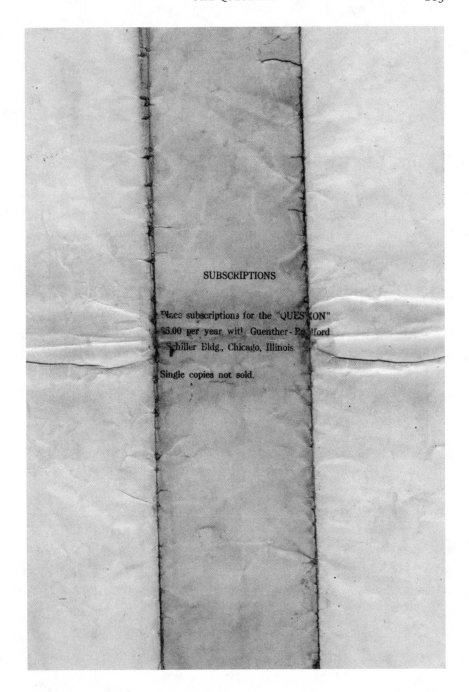

SUBSCRIPTIONS

Place subscriptions for the "QUESTION" $5.00 per year with Guenther-Radford Schiller Bldg., Chicago, Illinois.

Single copies not sold.

NOTES

1. AN AUSPICIOUS BEGINNING

1. "John W. Talbot Dies in Fire," *South Bend (IN) Tribune*, December 15, 1937.

2. "The Next Census," *National Union* (South Bend, IN), December 25, 1869.

3. Baptism of John Joseph Talbot, Sacred Heart Parish (Notre Dame, IN), microfilmed records of the Diocese of South Bend–Fort Wayne, LDS film 1617239, item 3. Hannah's maiden name was Talbot, but it does not appear that she was a close relative of her husband.

4. *Annual Catalogue* (Notre Dame, IN: University of Notre Dame Press, 1883), http://archives.nd.edu/bulletin/AC_39.pdf.

5. *Annual Catalogue* (Notre Dame, IN: University of Notre Dame Press, 1861), http://archives.nd.edu/bulletin/AC_17.pdf.

6. Entry for Peter Talbot in "Index to Early Notre Dame Students," University of Notre Dame Archives, accessed January 31, 2018, http://archives.nd.edu/search/students.htm. Manual labor students were generally either very poor or orphaned.

7. Entry for Hannah Talbot, 1900 U.S. Federal Census, South Bend, St. Joseph, IN, Enumeration District 128, roll T623 1240402, 5.

8. Baptism of Joseph Edward Talbot, St. Joseph Parish (South Bend, IN), microfilmed records of the Diocese of South Bend–Fort Wayne, LDS film 1617235, item 3, 32. The family had attended church at Notre Dame's Sacred Heart, but a new church, St. Joseph's, had formed just south of where they lived, and the later children were baptized there.

9. Interment of Mary Talbot, St. Joseph Parish (South Bend, IN), microfilmed records of the Diocese of South Bend–Fort Wayne, LDS film 1617235, item 4, 320.

10. Last will and testament of Peter Talbot, May 28, 1880, St. Joseph County Archives, South Bend, IN; probate of Peter Talbot, 1880, St. Joseph County Archives, South Bend, IN.

11. [John Talbot], "Come Again," *Owl*, October 25, 1917, 6, https://michiana-memory.sjcpl.org/digital/collection/p16827coll3/id/2892/rec/3.

12. [Talbot], "Come Again."

13. John Talbot, *Old Maid Ryan* (South Bend, IN: Owl Jewelry, ca. 1910), 3. Old Maid Ryan appears to have a basis in fact. Elizabeth Ryan, never married, ran a millinery store for many years near Talbot's office and was the same age as his subject. Talbot writes that Old Maid Ryan sold cemetery plots for a realty company. Elizabeth Ryan's obituary mentions that after closing her store she worked in real estate. Ryan died in 1928 at the age of seventy-eight.

14. Talbot, *Old Maid Ryan*, 3.

15. Student files of John and Joseph Talbot, University of Notre Dame Archives, Notre Dame, IN.

16. Last will and testament of Catherine Talbot, signed November 10, 1886, Indiana, Wills and Probate Records, 1798–1999, Will Book 1, 1889–1893, 113, https://www.ancestry.com.

17. Matrimonial, *South Bend (IN) Times*, September 26, 1895. John's aunt Katherine on his mother's side had married Phillip Letourneau and moved to Detroit. Although she died in 1886, his uncle and cousins were still there.

18. Michigan State Legislature 1895, Public Act 205, Library of Michigan Law Library, Lansing, MI.

19. Andrew Howell, *Annotated Statutes of 1882*, Library of Michigan Law Library, Lansing, MI.

20. A current definition of good character can be found in Diane Van Aken's, *Unravelling the Mystery of the Character and Fitness Process*, State Bar of Michigan, accessed December 6, 2018, https://www.michbar.org/file/professional/pdfs/unraveling.pdf.

21. Howell, *Annotated Statutes of 1882*, sec. 27.

22. "The Court News," *Detroit Free Press*, November 19, 1892.

23. An 1892 real estate ad in the *Detroit Free Press* listing John W. Talbot as a contact gives an address of room 20 in the McGraw Building. An 1892 Detroit directory shows lawyers M. P. McGregor and W. H. Woodbury at that address as well.

24. Today the Detroit College of Law is the Michigan State University College of Law.

25. Real estate classifieds, *Detroit Free Press*, September 27, 1892.

26. Matrimonial, *South Bend (IN) Times*, September 26, 1895.

27. Marriage of John W. Talbot and Mary O'Brien, Holy Trinity Parish, Diocese of Detroit, MI.

28. Baptism of John Harold Talbot, St. Joseph Parish (South Bend, IN), microfilmed records of the Diocese of South Bend–Fort Wayne, LDS film 1617235, item 6.

2. A BUDDING CAREER AND A BLOSSOMING CRIMINAL

1. Matrimonials, *South Bend (IN) Times,* September 26, 1895.

2. "Lawyer Sells Stolen Silks," *Chicago Tribune,* November 5, 1897.

3. "A Second Indictment," *Goshen (IN) Daily News,* November 8, 1897.

4. *Illustrated Fashion Catalogue: Summer, 1890* (New York: Bloomingdale's, 1890), 31, https://babel.hathitrust.org/cgi/pt?id=nnc2.ark:/13960/t5hb1f95g&view=1up&seq=1.

5. "Verdict in Thirteen Minutes: Jury at Plymouth, Ind., Acquits John W. Talbot of the Charge of Receiving Stolen Goods." *Kansas City (MO) Journal,* January 25, 1898.

6. "Brings Disagreeable Charges," *South Bend (IN) Tribune,* December 20, 1897.

7. "Desperate Men Out of Prison . . . Made a Specialty of Silks," *LaPorte (IN) Weekly Herald,* August 11, 1904.

8. "Lawyer Sells Stolen Silks," *Chicago Tribune,* November 5, 1897.

9. "Goshen's Carnival of Crime," *Richmond (IN) Daily Palladium,* September 20, 1904.

10. "Armed and Masked Highwaymen Operate on Moving Freight Train," *Bemidji (MN) Daily Pioneer,* July 6, 1904.

11. "Cleveland Patrolman Is Bound, Gagged, and Robbed by a Gang of Crooks," *Evening Bulletin* (Maysville, KY), April 4, 1900.

12. "The Lake Shore Gang," *Elyria (OH) Reporter,* October 12, 1899.

13. "Regular System: It Seems That Topeka Joe and His Pals Had Things Very Nicely Fixed for Their Work," *Adrian (MI) Daily Telegram,* August 2, 1901.

14. "A New Plat Opened," *South Bend (IN) Tribune,* August 27, 1898.

15. "State Rests Case: Defense Tries to Prove Alibi" *South Bend (IN) Tribune,* May 4, 1899. While on the stand, witness Alice Lemm had to swear that "she had never met Talbot at any saloon," implying that the prosecution claimed Talbot had approached her privately outside of the courtroom.

16. "Books Were Fixed: New Evidence in the Trial of Slater and Ellison," *Detroit Free Press,* May 7, 1899.

17. One of John Talbot's mistresses would later claim that she was with him when he visited the prison and arranged for the escape.

18. "Watching for Slater's Gang," *Detroit Free Press,* August 16, 1904.

19. "Regular System"

20. Leona Mason, *The Character and Life of John W. Talbot, Supreme President Order of Owls, Exposed by an Outraged Woman, One of His Victims* (South Bend, IN: printed by author, 1909).

21. "Wyatt Turned the Eagle Loose," *Bremen (IN) Enquirer,* July 6, 1900.

22. "Unusual Ceremony," *Fort Wayne (IN) Daily News,* January 1, 1902.

23. Anderson & Cooley, ed., *South Bend and the Men Who Have Made It* (South Bend, IN: Tribune Printing, 1901), 283.

24. Jos. E. Talbot to Rev. Andrew Morrissey, April 14, 1900, student file of Joseph Talbot, University of Notre Dame Archives, Notre Dame, IN.

25. Joseph E. Talbot, *South Bend (IN) Tribune*, November 3, 1906.

26. Marriage of Joseph Talbot and Edith Thompson, St. Joseph Parish (South Bend, IN), microfilmed records of the Diocese of South Bend–Fort Wayne, LDS film 1617239, item 8.

27. Mason, "Character and Life," 11.

28. "No Romance in Crime," *Indianapolis (IN) News*, July 4, 1919.

29. "Work Smooth Game," *South Bend (IN) Tribune*, April 7, 1908.

30. Mason, "Character and Life," 11.

3. DIVERSIFICATION: SOCIAL NETWORKS, POLITICAL INFLUENCE, AND THE IMPORTANCE OF FAMILY

1. Minor heirs of Dennis Clifford, St. Joseph County Guardianships, box 45, County Records of Indiana Microfilm Project (CRIMP), roll 432; microfilm held at St. Joseph County Public Library; originals held at St. Joseph County Archives, South Bend, IN.

2. "Death Summons P. J. Clifford," *South Bend (IN) Tribune*, December 7, 1927.

3. Although Fogarty was guilty of many of the things claimed by his opponents, he also advanced the city's interests. It was during his tenure that the promotional phrase "South Bend—World Famed" was created, and industrial growth, large-scale public works, and a wide-reaching reputation for the city were among his accomplishments. See *South Bend—World Famed* (South Bend, IN: South Bend Central Labor Union, 1909).

4. "Police Called Early to Quell Vote Troubles," *South Bend (IN) Tribune*, November 6, 1917.

5. "Death Summons P. J. Clifford."

6. "Joseph A. Luther Is Found Dead," *South Bend (IN) Tribune*, December 18, 1924.

7. "To Suppress Vice," *South Bend (IN) Tribune*, November 11, 1905.

8. "Seek to Enjoin Property Owners," *South Bend (IN) Tribune*, August 1, 1908.

9. John J. Hayes, *Thirty Years History of the Ancient Order of Hibernians, South Bend, Indiana: Division No. 1, January 11th, 1885, to January 11th, 1915* (New Carlisle, IN: E. L. Maudlin, ca. 1915), 5.

10. "In Memory of Emmett," *South Bend (IN) Tribune*, March 5, 1901.

11. John regularly wrote about religious tolerance. After his death, he had a secular funeral and was buried in the mainly protestant City Cemetery. In contrast, Joseph attended St. Joseph Catholic Church throughout his life; it was where his funeral took place. He was buried at Cedar Grove, a Catholic cemetery on the grounds of the University of Notre Dame.

12. Hayes, "Thirty Years," 14.

13. "Hoo! Hoo! Head Owls Are Coming!," *Detroit Free Press*, October 3, 1909.

4. THE FOUNDING OF THE ORDER OF OWLS

1. [John Talbot], Order of Owls promotional pamphlet (South Bend, IN: Order of Owls, ca. 1905). Held in the archival collection of St. Joseph County Public Library. James F. Dunbar died in February 1906 of tuberculosis.

2. John Talbot, *Who Is John Talbot?* (South Bend, IN: Order of Owls, 1909), 3. Only known copy held in the clipping files of the *South Bend Tribune*.

3. This motto appeared on letterhead, in ads, and on jewelry anywhere there were Owl nests. Talbot did not originate the phrase. The sentiment had been floating around for about a decade, appearing as a space filler in magazines and small newspapers such as the *Brown County World* without attribution. Spuriously credited to Robert Louis Stevenson, it was in fact used decades later by Thornton Wilder and James Truslow Adams. *The Oxford Dictionary of Quotations* credits it to Kansas governor Edward Wallis Hoch, through his newspaper, the *Marion Record*, but cannot date its first appearance in print and notes that he disavowed it. An early *Boston Evening Transcript* article supports Hoch as the source. Talbot likely saw it in the *New York Times*, where it appeared just months before the Owls were founded, there credited to a Rev. Peter McQueen. The Owls certainly increased exposure to the short verse and claimed it as their own. *Oxford Dictionary of Quotations*, ed. Elizabeth Knowles (Oxford: Oxford University Press, 2004), 19; *Brown County World*, Hiawatha KS, August 14, 1896; "Notes and Queries," *Boston Evening Transcript*, June 10, 1905; *New York Times*, February 14, 1904.

4. *Constitution & By-Laws—Lewiston Nest 1185* (Lewiston, PA: Order of Owls, 1948).

5. They hoped that the threat of higher initiation fees for members joining later would motivate prospects to join early.

6. John Talbot, *Old Maid Ryan* (South Bend, IN: Owl Jewelry Co., ca. 1910), 14.

7. The County Records of Indiana Microfilm Project (CRIMP), rolls 48 and 49, and miscellaneous records in the St. Joseph County Public Library include articles of association for other local fraternal orders. Indexes to the records go through 1910 and include entries for John Talbot in his role as an attorney but none for the Order of Owls, Owls, or John Talbot as a representative of the Owls.

8. Bill Loomis, "Clubbing in Days Past: When Fraternal Societies Ruled," *Detroit News*, October 10, 2015, https://www.detroitnews.com/story/news/local/michigan-history/2015/10/10/fraternal-societies-detroit-history/73514852/.

9. Order of Owls, *Catalogue of Lodge Equipment, Aids to Initiation, Advertising Novelties, Jewelry, Emblems, Prizes, Etc.* (South Bend, IN: Owl Jewelry, ca. 1910).

10. Talbot, *Who Is John Talbot?*, 4.

11. John W. Talbot, "The New Profession," included as exhibit 4, John W. Talbot v. the United States of America, case 3103, Seventh District Court of Appeals, 1921. Record held at the National Archives Chicago.

12. Talbot, *Who Is John Talbot?*, 4.

13. *Ritual: Order of Owls [Home Nest]* (South Bend, IN: Order of Owls, ca. 1905), 17. Held in the archival collection of the St. Joseph County Public Library, South Bend, IN.

14. "Owls Will Hoot for Many Mates," *Oxnard (CA) Courier,* July 2, 1909.

15. "Prospective Member Becomes Frightened at Initiation Ceremonies," *South Bend (IN) Daily Times,* February 3, 1907.

16. "Takes Owl Charter Away: Supreme President Talbot Puts Chattanooga Nest Out of Existence," *South Bend (IN) Daily Times,* July 15, 1908.

17. "Severe Injuries Sustained by John Maxwell in Initiatory Work," *Lima (OH) Times-Democrat,* May 19, 1909.

18. Greg Hoersten, "Order of Owls," April 19, 2016, https://www.limaohio.com /features/lifestyle/177329/order-of-owls.

19. Loomis, "Clubbing in Days Past."

20. "Owl Show Drives Woman Insane," *South Bend (IN) Tribune,* July 1, 1910.

21. "Owl's President Arrested on a Charge of Slander," *Union County Journal* (Marysville, OH), March 30, 1916.

22. *"National Order Owls Will Not Permit Burlesque Order," Morning Avalanche* (Lubbock, TX), September 12, 1925.

23. This cane is now in the collection of the History Museum in South Bend, Indiana.

5. LEGAL TROUBLE: THE TALBOT BROTHERS ON THE DEFENSIVE

1. "Disbarment Case Begins," *Goshen (IN) Democrat,* January 17, 1906.

2. "Nature of Indictment: Filed against Trio of Attorneys," *Plymouth (IN) Tribune,* April 13, 1905.

3. "Disbarment Case Begins."

4. "Owls Feast and Talk: First Annual Banquet of Order Is a Success," *South Bend (IN) Tribune,* September 23, 1905.

5. "Major [*sic*] Darrow Guilty of Professional Misconduct—Attorney Talbot Was Also Convicted," *Richmond (IN) Daily Palladium,* January 22, 1906.

6. "Talbot Loses in Disbarment Case," *South Bend (IN) Tribune,* July 1, 1910.

7. "Strong Charges against Talbot: Committee Makes Report to Judge Funk; Prosecutor Is on Grill," *South Bend (IN) Tribune,* September 15, 1908.

8. Madge Cole's establishment just happened to be located across the street from the Talbot brothers' office. One witness claimed the Talbots were part owners of the business.

9. "Talbot Trial Set," *South Bend (IN) Weekly Times,* October 9, 1908.

10. "Two New Charges against J. E. Talbot: Efforts to Influence Jury Commissioners Alleged," *South Bend (IN) Tribune,* October 10, 1908.

11. *South Bend (IN) Weekly Times,* October 13, 1908.

12. "A Personal Statement," *South Bend (IN) Weekly Times,* October 20, 1908.

13. Leona Mason, *The Character and Life of John W. Talbot, Supreme President Order of Owls, Exposed by an Outraged Woman, One of His Victims* (South Bend, IN: printed by author, 1909), 11.

14. "The Talbot Verdict," *South Bend (IN) Weekly Tribune*, February 27, 1909.

6. LEONA MASON TRIES TO PUT HIM DOWN

1. Leona Mason, *The Character and Life of John W. Talbot, Supreme President Order of Owls, Exposed by an Outraged Woman, One of His Victims* (South Bend, IN: printed by author, 1909), 8.

2. Leona's claim is substantiated by an article that notes that on a visit to Davenport, Iowa, "Mr. Talbot will be accompanied by his wife," *Daily Times* (Davenport, IA), June 30, 1908. Minnie was never known to travel with her husband.

3. Talbot famously rode this horse, Gopher, into a local tobacco shop to buy a cigar because he was in too much of a hurry to dismount.

4. Mason, *Character and Life*, 16.

5. Mason, *Character and Life*, 17.

6. Mason, *Character and Life*, 17.

7. John Talbot, *Who Is John Talbot?* (South Bend, IN: Order of Owls, 1909). Only known copy held in the clipping files of the *South Bend Tribune*.

8. "'Too Pretty' to Punish," *Muncie (IN) Morning Star Press*, June 24, 1909.

9. "Says John Talbot Abused Mrs. Mason," *South Bend (IN) Tribune*, October 5, 1909.

10. "Took Photo as She Was Nude," *Los Angeles Daily Times*, October 14, 1909.

11. There are no extant court records from this trial. The St. Joseph County Archives serves as the repository for records of this period, and staff there believe many were destroyed in paper drives during World War II. Events described here are gleaned from the daily press coverage of the trial.

12. "Leona Mason Married to Divorced Husband?," *South Bend (IN) Tribune*, July 1, 1910.

7. DEATH AND RESURRECTION

1. "Woman Sues for $25,000," *Fort Wayne (IN) Journal Gazette*, November 23, 1910.

2. "Joseph Talbot in Bad Condition," *Elkhart Daily (IN) Review*, July 1, 1910.

3. "Sent to Detroit: Joseph E. Talbot Taken into Custody at South Bend," *Goshen (IN) Democrat*, July 8, 1910.

4. John Frith, "Syphilis—Its Early History and Treatment until Penicillin and the Debate on Its Origins," *Journal of Military and Veterans' Health* 20, no. 4 (2012), https://jmvh.org/article/syphilis-its-early-history-and-treatment-until-penicillin-and-the-debate-on-its-origins/.

5. "Joseph E. Talbot Dies at Kenosha." *South Bend (IN) Tribune*, November 3, 1910.

6. Death certificate of Joseph E. Talbot, November 3, 1910, Wisconsin Department of Health, uncertified copy in possession of author. The cause of death is listed as "general paresis," a term referring to a specific condition causing death in late-stage syphilitic patients.

7. John J. Hayes, *Thirty Years History of the Ancient Order of Hibernians, South Bend, Indiana: Division No. 1, January 11th, 1885, to January 11th, 1915* (New Carlisle, IN: E. L. Maudlin, ca. 1915), 64.

8. Joseph Talbot is buried in Cedar Grove Cemetery, Notre Dame, Indiana.

9. "Name Committee to Fight Talbot's Admission to Bar: Bribery and Forgery Are New Charges," *South Bend (IN) News-Times,* June 9, 1914, 1.

10. "Name Committee to Fight Talbot's Admission."

11. "Talbot's Case to Come Up Friday," *South Bend (IN) Tribune,* June 11, 1914.

12. "New Committee to Oppose J. W. Talbot," *South Bend (IN) Tribune,* September 25, 1914.

13. "Gained Notoriety," *Indianapolis (IN) News,* November 16, 1918.

14. "Talbot Files Petition," *South Bend (IN) News-Times,* June 19, 1915.

15. "Wants to Be Reinstated," *Muncie (IN) Star Press,* July 15, 1915.

16. "John Talbot Asks Admission to Bar," *South Bend (IN) Tribune,* July 2, 1915.

17. "Ford Not to Hear John Talbot Case," *South Bend (IN) Tribune,* September 30, 1915.

18. "Attorneys May Desert Talbot," *South Bend (IN) News-Times,* November 8, 1915.

19. Tuthill was a Masonic grand master. "Judge Tuthill Will Hear Talbot Petition," *South Bend (IN) News-Times,* October 9, 1916.

20. "Charges Talbot Works in County: Attorney F. J. L. Meyer Appears against Owl Head in Fight for Readmission to the Bar," *South Bend (IN) News-Times,* October 13, 1916.

21. "Change of Venue Is Granted John Talbot," *South Bend (IN) News-Times,* March 5, 1917.

22. "Circuit Court News," *Rochester (IN) Weekly Republican,* November 15, 1917.

23. "J. F. [*sic*] Talbot Reinstated: Disbarred South Bend Lawyer May Practice in Courts Again," *Indianapolis (IN) News,* November 8, 1917.

24. "Reinstatement of John W. Talbot Was Brought About," *Goshen (IN) Democrat,* November 16, 1917; "Talbot Is Reinstated," *South Bend (IN) Tribune,* November 7, 1917.

8. UNWANTED OWLS

1. *Constitution & By-Laws—Lewiston Nest 1185* (Lewiston, PA: Order of Owls, 1948).

2. For a description of the company's offering, see "At the Court Street," *Buffalo (NY) Courier,* September 16, 1895.

3. Afro-American Order of Owls ad, *Freeman* (Indianapolis, IN), December 24, 1910.

4. "No Negro Owls There, Says Higher Hooter," *Atlanta Georgian and News*, June 13, 1911; Georgia Historic Newspapers database, https://gahistoricnewspapers .galileo.usg.edu/; "Dr. Lewis to Speak," *South Bend (IN) Tribune*, September 2, 1912.

5. "Annual Conference Done," *New York Age*, March 23, 1911.

6. William H. Perkins Jr., *Reports of Cases Argued and Adjudged in the Court of Appeals of Maryland* (Baltimore: King Bros., 1914), 473.

7. Perkins, *Reports of Cases*, 474.

8. "Proceeding before Judge Duffy," *Daily Record* (Baltimore, MD), October 2, 1913.

9. "A. A. O. Owls Win a Big Victory," *Afro American Ledger* (Baltimore, MD), July 4, 1914.

10. John W. Talbot et al. v. Afro-American Order of Owls, Baltimore Circuit Court, 1913; Afro-American Order of Owls Baltimore Nest 1 v. John W. Talbot, Court of Appeals of Maryland, 1914; https://casetext.com/case/afro-am-owls-v -talbot.

11. "Something New," *Indianapolis (IN) Recorder*, September 21, 1912.

12. M. C. Ohnesorge to "Dear Brother," January 10, 1913; privately held.

13. South Bend native Schuyler Colfax, who was Speaker of the House under Abraham Lincoln, spoke out regularly on the evils of slavery.

14. John W. Talbot to Ferdinand D'Esopo, October 13, 1937; privately held.

9. A PROFIT IN SYPHILIS

1. A summary included in a report done by the prison doctor at Leavenworth years later mentions these details but gives the year as 1914. Other reports list the date as March 1915.

2. Sarah Dunant, "Syphilis, Sex and Fear: How the French Disease Conquered the World," *Guardian* (London), May 17, 2013, https://www.theguardian.com /books/2013/may/17/syphilis-sex-fear-borgias.

3. John Frith, "Syphilis—Its Early History and Treatment until Penicillin and the Debate on Its Origins," *Journal of Military and Veterans' Health* 20, no. 4 (2012), https://jmvh.org/article/syphilis-its-early-history-and-treatment-until-penicillin- and-the-debate-on-its-origins/.

4. Testimony of John H. Talbot, *John W. Talbot v. the United States of America*, case 3103, Seventh District Court of Appeals, 1921. Record held at the National Archives Chicago.

5. Testimony of Edith Greif, *John W. Talbot v. the United States*.

6. Testimony of Edith Greif, *John W. Talbot v. the United States*.

7. Report of A. F. Yohe, prison physician to W. I. Biddle, warden, November 20, 1924, Leavenworth prison file of John Talbot 19003, National Archives Kansas City.

8. Report of A. F. Yohe, prison physician to W. I. Biddle, warden, January 20, 1924, Leavenworth prison file of John Talbot 19003, National Archives Kansas City.

9. However, there were apparently lasting effects. After this time, according to his son, Talbot was "very, very excitable and very nervous." Testimony of John H. Talbot, *John Talbot v. the United States.*

10. Amanda Yarnell, "Salvarsan," *Chemical and Engineering News,* June 20, 2005, https://pubs.acs.org/cen/coverstory/83/8325/8325salvarsan.html.

11. "Profit on Corner in Drug Depends on Sea Blockade," *Chicago Tribune,* November 25, 1915.

12. "Drug Prices Advance to Enormous Figures," *Daily News-Record* (Harrisonburg, VA), October 22, 1915.

13. "Scores Dying Here for Want of Salvarsan," *Kokomo (IN) Daily Tribune,* November 16, 1915.

14. "Salvarsan Released," *Staunton (VA) Daily Leader,* November 19, 1915.

15. "Profit on Corner in Drug."

16. Testimony of Pearl Spangler, *John Talbot v. the United States.* Spangler testified that she had stayed at the Talbot family home because Talbot's wife and son were living in Bloomington while he was attending school.

17. "Soldier Boys Think of Old I.U.," *Daily Student* (Bloomington, IN), August 4, 1916.

18. Indiana University, *Arbutus* (Bloomington: Indiana University, 1916, 1918, 1919).

19. "Fourteen Elected to Phi Beta Kappa," *Daily Student* (Bloomington, IN), May 27, 1919.

10. AN OWL REBELLION AND THE CHARITABLE
INSTITUTIONS THAT WEREN'T

1. "Owls' Lodges May Engage in Warfare: Members of Order Anxiously Await Reports: Finances Are Probed," *South Bend (IN) Tribune,* August 7, 1912.

2. The November 1911 issue of the *Owl* includes October's monthly expenses, amounting to approximately $5,000. However, without details on the income, it is impossible to understand these numbers. An example of how complicated it could be to make sense of the information includes this example: multiple payments labeled "Stenographer" add up to $240. According to the historical statistics of the Federal Reserve Archival System for Economic Research, South Bend's average pay for this type of work was forty dollars per month, so this would imply that the

Owls employed six full-time stenographers, which seems excessive. Of course, another possibility is that this was John's way of funneling money to his mistresses.

3. John Talbot, *Who Is John Talbot?* (South Bend, IN: Order of Owls, 1909), 7. Only known copy held in the clipping files of the *South Bend Tribune*.

4. Ruth Dorrel, "Newspaper Articles from St. Joseph County, 1912," *Hoosier Genealogist*, Indiana Historical Society, June 2001. The "tragic accident" was that Samuel shot his wife for being flirtatious with another man and was killed in retaliation.

5. "Owl Orphans Given Entertainment and Gifts," *South Bend (IN) Tribune*, December 30, 1914.

6. "Owls Sued by Orphans' Home on $2866 Bill," *South Bend (IN) Tribune*, March 21, 1933. By the age of seventeen, Victor was back in Illinois, working in a coal mine.

7. Testimony of Mary Ohnesorge, *John W. Talbot v. the United States of America*, case 3103, Seventh District Court of Appeals, 1921. Record held at the National Archives Chicago.

8. "Owl Hospital Is Assured: Dr. J. W. Hill Goes East to Purchase Equipment for Institution," *South Bend (IN) Tribune*, June 12, 1912. The South Bend hospital was not the only such proposed facility. Owl literature refers to Owl-run tuberculosis hospitals in Vermont and Colorado, but there is no evidence that planning for either of these facilities ever reached fruition. For the Vermont site, there is no record of the fourteen-hundred-acre land purchase claimed, and the location, in Gaysville, would have been almost inaccessible and the tiny town unable to support a large hospital. Also, the desirability of tuberculosis institutions was a volatile topic in Vermont during this period. Details for the Colorado institution mentioned are so sparse as to be impossible to investigate.

9. St. Joseph Hospital is still in existence today, although it moved from its original location in 2015.

10. "Expect Talbot Case to Go to Jurors Today," *South Bend (IN) News-Times*, November 23, 1921.

11. Testimony of Pearl Spangler, *John W. Talbot v. the United States*; Prosecutor Van Nuys, *John W. Talbot v. the United States*.

12. Letter from M. B. Keegan to W. I. Biddle, June 27, 1923, Leavenworth prison file of John Talbot #19003, National Archives Kansas City

13. By this point, Frank W. Bailey, a local printer, had been an Owl officer for years. His business was just a few doors from the Owl headquarters, and Talbot undoubtedly made use of his services.

14. Testimony of E. J. Freyermuth, *John W. Talbot v. the United States*; Prosecutor Van Nuys, *John W. Talbot v. the United States*.

15. Mary Ohnesorge testified to that number in court.

16. "Libel Suit Case Disposed of Today," *Brazil (IN) Daily Times*, April 10, 1920.

17. Asst. Chaplain H. H. Clark to Asst. Attorney General William Donovan, February 3, 1925, Leavenworth prison File of John Talbot #19003, National Archives Kansas City.

18. "Wants Receivership for Order of Owls," *South Bend (IN) Tribune*, February 3, 1914. This estimate was made by Jonas Hoover, an attorney who had worked for the home nest. Owls in South Carolina calculated that the number was more than double that, almost $150,000. "Owls Can't Live in Carolina," *Atlanta Constitution*, May 23, 1911.

19. "The Fraternal Order of Eagles Diabetic Research Center," Fraternal Order of Eagles, n.d., accessed August 24, 2018, https://www.foe.com/Charities /Diabetes-Research-Center.

11. CAN'T KEEP OUT OF TROUBLE AND OTHER ODD BEHAVIOR

1. "Talbot Gives Self Up: Head of Owls Charged with Assault on John E. Fisher," *South Bend (IN) Tribune*, June 24, 1912.

2. Existing local case files are held by the St. Joseph County Archives, South Bend, IN. Archives staff believe that many early paper files were destroyed during paper drives during World War II. A few cases survive on microfilm, but this is not one of them.

3. Emily Dickinson, "Tell All the Truth but Tell It Slant," *The Poems of Emily Dickinson: Reading Edition* (Harvard: Belknap Press, 1998).

4. F. J. Lewis Meyer v. John W. Talbot, St. Joseph County Circuit Court, cause #1192, St. Joseph County Archives, South Bend, IN.

5. "Meyer-Talbot Case Bitterly Fought," *South Bend (IN) Tribune*, February 3, 1913.

6. "Marshall Says He'll Not Mix in Talbot Case," *South Bend (IN) News-Times*, March 18, 1916.

7. The author of the piece was Thomas McCabe, who had been employed by the Moose to work at the Mooseheart facility.

8. See http://www.mooseheart.org/, accessed January 25, 2018.

9. "John Talbot and Alf. Martin Train Vice and G.O.P. Joint Guns on Ackerman Ancestry: Talbot Insists Defense Is Akin to Treason," *South Bend (IN) News-Times*, October 19, 1917.

10. "John Talbot and Alf. Martin."

11. "Carson Wins," *South Bend (IN) Tribune*, November 7, 1917.

12. "Talbot Assaulted Again," *Daily Gate City and Constitution-Democrat* (Keokuk, IA), May 22, 1919.

13. "Attempt to Kill J. W. Talbot Fails: Attorney Felled to Sidewalk by Unidentified Man," *South Bend (IN) Tribune*, May 22, 1919.

14. "John W. Talbot Beaten Up Again Reply to Letter," *South Bend (IN) News-Times*, September 26, 1919.

12. NOT JUST OWLS: TALBOT CULTIVATES AN INTEREST IN EXOTIC BIRDS (THE KIND WITH FEATHERS)

1. Helen H. Bartlett v. Glenn C. Bartlett, Michigan, filed July 20, 1909, Divorce Records, 1897–1952, 1908 Otsego–1910 Jackson, 61, https://www.ancestry.com.

2. Divorce decree, Helen H. Bartlett vs. Glenn C. Bartlett, September 27, 1909, Cass County, MI, Circuit Court File Room. According to the clerk, no other documents from the divorce proceedings survive.

3. "Rare Birds Shown at Niles Poultry Show," *South Bend (IN) News-Times*, December 19, 1913.

4. It seems clear that Helen introduced Talbot to exotic fowl, as he consistently elevates her over himself as an expert in all his public statements. Given Talbot's ego, his willingness to defer to her is an important clue to their dynamic.

5. Ralph Bartlett may also have kept birds, as a newspaper article about Cassopolis game-bird raising alludes to both Helen and her brother: "State Game Refuge," [*Niles (MI) Star?*], May 6, 1915. The article is included in a scrapbook Helen Bartlett assembled, currently in the possession of her relatives.

6. The cover gives the publisher's name as the Question Co., Indianapolis, but no record of this company exists. Guenther-Bradford had recently faced federal charges of libel and conspiracy for blackmailing businesses to pay for advertising in its publications. The fact that they were somehow allied with John Talbot suggests ties to the Chicago underworld. Louis Guenther v. the Ridgeway Company, New York Supreme Court Appellate Division, First Department, vol. 3281; "Louis Guenther and the Financial Underworld: How His Publication Was Conceived and Born; How He Has Used It to Procure Advertising and Sell Questionable Securities," *Magazine of Wall Street* 26, October 2, 1920.

7. *The Question* (Indianapolis, IN: Question Publishing, 1917). Talbot's Leavenworth file documents a one-inch scar on his thumb.

8. Indenture from George and Caroline Reum to Helen Bartlett and John W. Talbot, filed in Berrien County, MI, November 13, 1915.

9. Indenture from Margaret Susannah Decker to Helen Bartlett and John H. Talbot, filed in Berrien County, MI, July 24, 1917.

10. Sabine Farm is an interesting choice of names, given the reference to the rape of the Sabine women in Roman mythology.

11. *History of Berrien and Van Buren Counties, Michigan, with Illustrations and Biographical Sketches of Its Prominent Men and Pioneers* (Philadelphia: D. W. Ensign, 1880), 171.

12. "Leader of North American Indians Buys Niles Home for Headquarters," *South Bend (IN) Tribune*, August 21, 1929.

13. Quitclaim, John H. Talbot to Helen Bartlett and John W. Talbot, filed in Berrien County, MI, April 23, 1920.

14. In 1916, when the society was given as the publisher for one of Talbot's books, it is not listed in the South Bend city directory, despite showing a South Bend address. Talbot is the only individual ever to invoke its name, and no other record of its existence can be found.

15. "Peacocks Held Noblest of Birds," *Indianapolis (IN) Star,* January 15, 1916.

16. Pheasant postcard (Portland, OR: National Colortype, ca. 1917); John Talbot, "Pheasant Rearing and Hatching," *American Bantam Fancier* 2, no. 4, September 1914. It is possible that the postcard is another of Talbot's printed imposters. American Colortype Co. was a contemporary postcard printer in Chicago. National Colortype Co. operated out of Bellevue, Kentucky, but mainly printed signs.

17. "Why Not Raise Pheasants While You Are Raising Chickens?," *Montgomery (AL) Advertiser,* November 14, 1915.

18. "Mrs. Bartlett Will Talk at Notable Meet" and "Mrs. Bartlett Leaves Sunday for New York," no publications or dates; clippings included in a scrapbook Helen Bartlett assembled, currently in the possession of her relatives.

19. "Do You Know," *Niles (MI) Daily Star,* Niles Public Library Clipping File.

20. The Sisters of the Holy Cross originally resided in Bertrand, Michigan. They moved their mission to their current site, which includes St. Mary's College at Notre Dame, in 1855. This log cabin may have been moved with several other original buildings. If so, it was likely located near where Mother Pauline intended to build LeMans Hall, "one of the college's most notable landmarks." She promoted a new campus plan to the governors at the same time Helen was supposed to have purchased the cabin.

21. This structure was well known locally, and there was interest in treating it as an historic site. A 1979 historic survey held at the Niles Public Library in Niles, Michigan, referred to it as the "second oldest house in Niles." Unfortunately, a fire in 2000 burned it beyond repair, and the structure was dismantled: "Blaze Ends Dream of Restoring Historic Niles Log Cabin," *South Bend (IN) Tribune,* October 3, 2000.

22. John W. Talbot, *Game Laws and Game* (South Bend, IN: Game Bird Society, 1916), 12. Available at https://babel.hathitrust.org/cgi/pt?id=coo1.ark:/13960 /t50g4729n&view=1up&seq=7.

23. Talbot, *Game Laws,* 16.

24. Talbot, *Game Laws,* 20.

25. Michigan governor Woodbridge N. Ferris to Helen Bartlett, January 20, 1915; included in a scrapbook Helen Bartlett assembled, currently in the possession of her relatives.

26. A. M. Stoddart, "Ruffed Grouse in New York State: A Summary of an Investigation Made by the New York State Conservation Commission into the Causes for Their Decrease" (Albany: New York Conservation Commission, 1918).

27. "To Arraign Talbot at Capital on Nov. 25," *South Bend (IN) Tribune*, November 16, 1918. The issue of the *Owl* that contained the text was from April 16, 1917, but no copies of this issue appear to have survived.

28. United States of America v. John W. Talbot, Docket of the US District Court in Indianapolis, case 1590, National Archives Chicago.

13. "SHE IS CERTAINLY HAVING A FINE TIME"

1. "Scanlon in Court," *South Bend (IN) Tribune*, November 17, 1921.

2. "Unfolds Story of Degeneracy in Talbot Case," *South Bend (IN) News-Times*, November 21, 1921.

3. John Talbot to Pearl Bagley, September 24, 1920, John W. Talbot v. the United States of America, case 3103, Seventh District Court of Appeals, 1921. Record held at the National Archives Chicago.

4. Pearl Spangler was another former divorce client of Talbot's and his mistress. She was at least the third woman Talbot cultivated for a relationship in this manner.

5. "Seeks Jail Refuge from Owl Chieftain: Kansas Woman Describes House of Fear," *South Bend (IN) Tribune*, October 20, 1920.

6. Testimony of Pearl Bagley, *John W. Talbot v. the United States*.

7. According to Leona Mason's testimony at her trial ten years earlier, this door was often used to bring women in and out of Talbot's office without being seen.

8. John Talbot to William Bagley, October 13, 1920, *John W. Talbot v. the United States*.

9. Testimony of Pearl Bagley, *John W. Talbot v. the United States*.

10. John Talbot to William Bagley, October 15, 1920, *John W. Talbot v. the United States*.

11. William Bagley to Frank Gilmer, city court judge, October 23, 1920, *John W. Talbot v. the United States*.

12. Testimony of Jenny Penwell, jail matron, *John W. Talbot v. the United States*.

13. Classifieds: Woman—Stenographer, *Chicago Tribune*, July 6, 1921.

14. "Chief of Owls Taken on White Slave Charge," *Chicago Tribune*, February 26, 1921; "Owls' Chief is Held on Woman's Charge," *New York Times*, February 26, 1921.

15. "Witnesses Return from Talbot Trial," *South Bend (IN) News-Times*, November 23, 1921.

16. "Owls President Guilty of Violating Mann Act," *Fort Wayne (IN) Journal-Gazette*, November 24, 1921.

17. Testimony of Pearl Bagley, *John W. Talbot v. the United States*.

18. Testimony of Charles D. Humes, physician, *John W. Talbot v. the United States*.

19. Testimony of John A. McDonald, *John W. Talbot v. the United States*.

20. Testimony of Pearl Bagley, *John W. Talbot v. the United States.*

21. "Need for City Isolation Hospital Is Urgent Here," *South Bend (IN) News-Times,* November 13, 1921.

22. City News Briefs, *South Bend (IN) Tribune,* November 23, 1921.

23. "Talbot, Head of Owls, Guilty at Mann Act Trial," *Chicago Tribune,* November 25, 1921.

24. "Klan to Absorb Owls in Dixie, Organizer Declares," *Chicago Tribune,* December 30, 1922.

25. "Anderson Sentences Talbot 5 Years: Attorney Fined $5,000 also for 'Slave' Violation," *South Bend (IN) News-Times,* November 30, 1921.

26. "John Talbot Is on His Way: Head of Owls Slated for Waiting Cell," *South Bend (IN) Tribune,* March 2, 1923.

27. "50,000 Marchers in Jubilee Parade: Colorful Spectacle as Members of Fraternal Orders Move Down Fifth Avenue," *New York Times,* June 24, 1923.

14. "GUILTY AS SIN": TALBOT IS SENT TO LEAVENWORTH

1. On his release, the belongings Talbot had brought to prison with him were sent to Helen Bartlett. A penknife bearing Talbot's name, likely the one listed, is among Helen's possessions that her family continues to keep.

2. J. Gordon Bonine, MD, physician's supplementary report, n.d., Leavenworth prison file of John Talbot #19003, National Archives Kansas City.

3. Letter A. F. Yohe to W. I. Biddle, warden, January 2, 1925, Leavenworth file of John Talbot #19003.

4. Keegan had previously been Talbot's neighbor on Main Street. In earlier South Bend city directories, Keegan was listed as a druggist; in subsequent directories he was listed as a physician but at a different address. During the year of the trial and while in prison, Talbot clearly hoped Keegan's name would lend more credibility to the dubious operations of the Owl hospital.

5. Telegram John W. Talbot to E. B. Slusser, August 16, 1923, Leavenworth prison file of John Talbot #19003.

6. Correspondence report, Leavenworth prison file of John Talbot #19003.

7. Letter H. H. Clark to William Donovan, asst. attorney general, Washington, DC, Leavenworth prison file of John Talbot #19003.

8. Warrant for commutation of sentence of Albert Holtzman, 1914, GLC00045.39.01, Gilder Lehrman Institute of American History, https://www.gilderlehrman.org/collection-item-resource-creator/finch-james-fl-1914.

15. THE EX-CONVICT: TALBOT IS NO LONGER SUPREME

1. Property in storage index card, stamped May 10, 1925, Leavenworth prison file of John Talbot #19003, National Archives Kansas City.

2. Warden Biddle to H. C. Heckman, president, Board of Parole, February 16, 1926, Leavenworth prison file of John Talbot #19003.

3. Letters to Parole Officer Timmons from John D. Burke, February 20, 1926, and George M. Plattner, South Bend park commissioner, February 23, 1926, Leavenworth prison file of John Talbot #19003.

4. "J. W. Talbot Wins Third of Claims against Son," *South Bend (IN) Tribune,* May 28, 1927.

5. "Find Bomb in Owls' Building," *South Bend (IN) Tribune,* May 25, 1926.

6. "Plant Bomb in Talbot Building," *South Bend (IN) News-Times,* May 25, 1926.

7. "Find Bomb." In response to this event, South Bend public safety officials decided to form a bomb squad to deal with future emergencies of this type.

8. The complaint was signed Harry Brown, but the parole officer investigating could not find a person by this name in the area. Helen may have submitted the claim but was reluctant to sign her name to it.

9. Jno. A. Greif to N. R. Timmons, parole officer, February 25, 1926, Leavenworth prison file of John Talbot #19003. John Greif was John's sister-in-law's second husband and his sponsor after prison. John was supposed to be staying with them at the time.

10. Report of Linus P. Meredith, U.S. Marshal, February 9, 1926, Leavenworth prison file of John Talbot #19003.

11. N. R. Timmons to John W. Talbot, February 20, 1926, Leavenworth prison file of John Talbot #19003.

12. Helen Bartlett to Joseph E. Wartha, May 29, 1926, Michigan, County Marriage Records, 1822–1940, https://www.ancestry.com.

13. "Escapes Jail Sentence," *Indianapolis (IN) News,* July 7, 1920; "First Case Saturday," *South Bend (IN) News-Times,* June 26, 1920. Wartha had operated a kind of soda fountain a few blocks from Talbot's office that apparently also illegally served liquor. In his position as a deputy marshal, he had only months before been arresting those guilty of the same crime.

14. "John W. Talbot Missing, Disappears from South Bend: Lawyer Said to Be in Far-Western State," *South Bend (IN) Tribune,* December 5, 1927.

15. "Once Wealthy Lawyer Reported Missing," *Elwood (IN) Call Leader,* December 8, 1927.

16. "Talbot Said to Be Held," *Times* (Munster, IN), June 11, 1928.

17. John W. Talbot v. Helen Wartha, U.S. District Court, Western District of Michigan, 1927; "Case against Niles Woman is Dismissed," *Benton Harbor (MI) Herald Palladium,* May 16, 1928.

18. "Acquit Talbot of Perjury Charge: Former Head of Owls' Order Is Free Again," *South Bend (IN) Tribune,* October 11, 1928.

19. "Battle of Owls Will Be Resumed in Court," *South Bend (IN) Tribune,* February 9, 1928.

20. "Young Talbot Loses Rule over Owls," *South Bend (IN) Tribune,* March 27, 1929.

16. A QUIETER LIFE

1. Death record of Mary Katherine Ohnesorge, June 10, 1935, Michigan, U.S., Death Records, 1867–1950, https://www.ancestry.com.

2. These cousins were Margaret Luther, Joseph Luther, and Alice Luther. Alice's cause of death is shown on her death certificate.

3. In December 1911, John Luther killed his neighbor and friend Thomas Bauer with a blow to the head. Bauer's wife had fled to the Luther home in fear of her husband, and Luther claimed self-defense when the man with whom he had been out drinking a few hours before showed up on his doorstep in a rage.

4. "Dismiss Remaining Charges of Talbot," *South Bend (IN) Weekly Tribune*, October 23, 1909; "Talbot Unalarmed by Insanity Charge," *South Bend (IN) News-Times*, June 25, 1912; "Is Talbot Crazy? Proceedings Started against South Bend Lawyer," *Goshen (IN) Democrat*, June 28, 1912.

5. *Diagnostic and Statistical Manual of Mental Disorders*, 5th ed. (Arlington, VA: American Psychiatric Association, 2013).

6. Scott A. Bonn, "How to Tell a Sociopath from a Psychopath: Understanding Important Distinctions between Criminal Sociopaths and Psychopaths," *Psychology Today*, January 22, 2014, https://www.psychologytoday.com.

17. A FIERY DEATH

1. John W. Talbot to William Lowe Bryan, July 17, 1935, Indiana University Archives Collection C286.260.

2. William Lowe Bryan to John W. Talbot, July 19, 1935, Indiana University Archives Collection C286.260.

3. "John Talbot Is Dead in Fire," *South Bend (IN) Tribune*, December 15, 1937.

4. St. Joseph County, Indiana, coroner's inquest for John W. Talbot, D. Donald Grillo, coroner, filed December 28, 1937, St. Joseph County Archives, South Bend, IN.

5. "Burned to Death in Fire at Office," *Indianapolis (IN) Star*, December 16, 1937.

6. "Taken to Michigan City," *Starke County (IN) Republican*, October 17, 1907. Webb's lawyer would later defend Talbot on the Mann Act charge. This Frank Webb is not to be confused with the man of the same name incarcerated in Michigan City on a charge of petit larceny, who died in 1915.

7. Arthur Preuss, *A Dictionary of Secret and Other Societies: A Look at American Organizations, 1800–1920* (Washington, DC: Westphalia Press, 2015).

18. THE FATE OF THE ORDER OF OWLS

1. "The Mortuary Record: John J. Johnson," *South Bend (IN) Tribune*, December 13, 1912.

2. Ferdinand D'Esopo to John W. Talbot, October 13, 1937, privately held.

3. "Atty. Ferdinand D'Esopo Dies: Former Alderman," *Hartford (CT) Courant*, June 5, 1971.

4. "4 Accused of Wrecking Restaurant," *State* (Columbia, SC), August 11, 1961.

5. "Georgia Briefs," *Brunswick (GA) News*, September 13, 1962.

6. "Order of Owls Club Accused of Discrimination," *TriState (IN, KY, IL) Homepage*, September 19, 2015.

7. "Who We Are," Order of Eagles, accessed December 4, 2021, https://www.foe.com/About-The-Eagles/Who-We-Are; "Who We Are," Order of Elks, accessed August 24, 2018, https://www.elks.org/who/information.cfm.

8. "Who Are the Shriners?" Shriners International, https://www.shriners international.org/Shriners/History/Beginnings, accessed August 24, 2018.

9. "Order of Owls" in Tax Exempt Organization Search, Internal Revenue Service, accessed August 2018, https://apps.irs.gov/app/eos/.

19. TALBOT'S LEGACY

1. *The Question* (Indianapolis, IN: Question Publishing, 1917), 4.

2. Testimonial of Theodore Thorward, *Who Is John Talbot?* (South Bend, IN: Order of Owls, 1909). Only known copy held in the clipping files of the *South Bend Tribune*.

3. "Order of Owls Beaten in Case," *Daily Gate City* (Keokuk, IA), May 4, 1913.

4. John W. Talbot, *Old Maid Ryan* (South Bend, IN: Owl Jewelry Co., ca. 1910), 9–10.

5. Leona Mason, *The Character and Life of John W. Talbot, Supreme President Order of Owls, Exposed by an Outraged Woman, One of His Victims* (South Bend, IN: printed by author, 1909), 8.

6. Mason, *Character and Life*, 3.

20. POSTSCRIPT

1. Obituary of Miss Mary Ohnesorge, *South Bend (IN) Tribune*, June 21, 1935.

2. Pearl Spangler to Edwin Smith, May 6, 1904, Michigan, U.S., Marriage Records, 1867–1952, film 000945413, https://www.ancestry.com.

3. Edwin E. Smith v. Pearl Smith, divorce case 12310, filed April 19, 1908, St. Joseph County, held by the St. Joseph County Archives, South Bend, IN.

4. Death certificate of Pearl Spangler, May 28, 1938, Indiana Death Certificates, 1899–2011, https://www.ancestry.com.

5. Inquest for Pearl Spanger, St. Joseph County Coroner's Office, filed June 18, 1938, held by the St. Joseph County Archives, South Bend, IN.

6. "Gleaners Fraternity Contemplate Building Home for the Aged in Niles," *Niles (MI) Daily Star*, May 9, 1929.

7. "Leader of North American Indians Buys Niles Home for Headquarters," *South Bend (IN) Tribune*, August 21, 1929.

8. Helen B. Wartha to Dorothy De Poy, warranty deed, January 6, 1949, Berrien County, MI, held at the county courthouse in Niles, MI.

9. Helen Bartlett Wartha to the Berrien County Package Company, warranty deed, June 29, 1949, Berrien County, MI, held at the county courthouse in Niles, MI.

10. Obituary of Mrs. Helen Hain Wartha, *Niles (MI) Daily Star,* October 1, 1951.

11. Obituary of Mr. John A. Greif, *South Bend (IN) Tribune,* April 10, 1953.

12. Obituary of Mrs. Edith M. Greif, *South Bend (IN) Tribune,* February 4, 1959.

13. Obituary of Mrs. Mary Ellen Talbot, *South Bend (IN) Tribune,* December 22, 1955.

14. "The East Wayne Street Local Historic District," Historic Preservation Commission of South Bend and St. Joseph County, IN, 2018, https://southbendin .gov/wp-content/uploads/2018/07/Standards-and-Guidelines_East-Wayne -Street.pdf.

15. "Inspect New Branch Library for River Park Residents," *South Bend (IN) News-Times,* September 14, 1937.

16. Obituary of John H. Talbot, *South Bend (IN) Tribune,* June 15, 1967.

BIBLIOGRAPHY

Anderson & Cooley, ed. *South Bend and the Men Who Have Made It*. South Bend, IN: Tribune, 1901.

Barnard, Frederick A. *American Biographical History of Eminent and Self-Made Men: Michigan*, vol. 2. Cincinnati, OH: Western Biographical, 1878.

Bartlett, Helen. "Raising Pheasants on a Business Basis." *Country Life in America*, May 1915.

Beckley, Charles S. *South Bend Phizes and Pointers*. South Bend, IN: printed by author, ca. 1912.

Loomis, Bill. "Clubbing in Days Past: When Fraternal Societies Ruled." *Detroit News*, October 10, 2015.

Lutholtz, M. William. *Grand Dragon: D. C. Stephenson and the Ku Klux Klan in Indiana*. West Lafayette, IN: Purdue Research Foundation, 1991.

Mason, Leona. *The Character and Life of John W. Talbot, Supreme President Order of Owls, Exposed by an Outraged Woman, One of His Victims*. South Bend, IN: printed by author, 1909.

Order of Owls, *Catalogue of Lodge Equipment, Aids to Initiation, Advertising Novelties, Jewelry, Emblems, Prizes, Etc. Etc.* South Bend, IN: Home Nest Order of Owls, ca. 1910.

Preuss, Arthur. *A Dictionary of Secret and Other Societies*. Detroit: Gale Research, 1966.

The Question. Indianapolis, IN: Question Publishing, 1917.

South Bend—World Famed. South Bend, IN: South Bend Central Labor Union, 1909.

South Bend, World Famed. South Bend, IN: Handelsman & Young, 1922.

Talbot, John. *Who Is John Talbot?* South Bend, IN: Order of Owls, 1909.

——. *Old Maid Ryan*. South Bend, IN: Owl Publishing, ca. 1911.

——. "Pheasant Rearing and Hatching." *American Bantam Fancier* 2, no. 4, September 1914.

——. *Game Laws and Game*. South Bend, IN: Game Bird Society, 1916.

Whalen, William J. *Handbook of Secret Organizations*. Milwaukee: Bruce Publishing, 1966.

INDEX